The Art of Team work

Building Stronger Bonds and Achieving Victory Together

Chris Black

© Copyright 2024 by Chris Black
All Rights Reserved

The presentation of the information is without contract or any type of guarantee assurance. The trademarks that are used are without any consent, and the publication of the trademark is without permission or backing by the trademark owner. All trademarks and brands within this book are for clarifying purposes only and are the owned by the owners themselves, not affiliated with this document.

Table of Contents

Chapter 1

Understanding Team Dynamics

The Essence of Teamwork

Teamwork is the invisible thread that weaves individuals into a cohesive unit, transforming disparate talents and personalities into a harmonious force capable of achieving remarkable feats. At its core, teamwork is about synergy—the idea that the collective power of a group surpasses the sum of its individual parts. This essence of teamwork is not merely about working together; it is about creating an environment where collaboration thrives, where each member feels valued, and where the shared goal becomes a beacon guiding every action.

The foundation of effective teamwork lies in understanding the unique strengths and weaknesses of each team member. Recognizing that every individual brings something distinct to the table is crucial. Whether it's analytical prowess, creative flair, or exceptional organizational skills, these diverse attributes must be harnessed and aligned with the team's objectives. This alignment requires a keen awareness of each member's capabilities and a willingness to adapt roles and responsibilities to maximize the team's potential.

A successful team operates much like a well-oiled machine, where each component plays a vital role in the overall function. However, unlike machines, teams are composed of human beings with emotions, aspirations, and personal challenges. This human element introduces a dynamic complexity that requires careful navigation. Empathy and understanding become essential tools in fostering a supportive environment where team members feel comfortable expressing their ideas and concerns.

Communication is the lifeblood of any team. It is the conduit through which ideas flow, decisions are made, and conflicts are resolved. Effective communication goes beyond the mere exchange of information; it involves active listening, open dialogue, and the ability to convey thoughts clearly and concisely. In a team setting, communication must be inclusive, ensuring that every voice is heard and respected. This inclusivity not only enhances decision-making but also strengthens the bonds between team members, fostering a sense of belonging and mutual respect.

Trust is the cornerstone upon which the edifice of teamwork is built. Without trust, collaboration falters, and the team becomes a collection of individuals working in silos. Building trust requires time, consistency, and transparency. It involves demonstrating reliability, keeping commitments, and being honest about challenges and limitations. Trust is a two-way street; it demands that team members have faith in each other's abilities and intentions, creating a safe space where vulnerability is not seen as a weakness but as an opportunity for growth.

Conflict is an inevitable aspect of teamwork, arising from differing perspectives, priorities, and personalities. However, when managed constructively, conflict can be a catalyst for innovation and improvement. The key lies in approaching disagreements with an open mind and a focus on finding solutions rather than assigning blame. Encouraging a culture of constructive criticism, where feedback is given and received with the intent to improve, can transform potential conflicts into opportunities for learning and development.

The essence of teamwork also involves a shared vision—a common goal that unites the team and provides direction. This vision must be clearly articulated and embraced by all members, serving as a guiding star that aligns efforts and motivates action. A shared vision fosters a sense of purpose, reminding team members that their contributions are part of something larger than themselves. It instills a sense of pride and ownership, driving individuals to go above and beyond in pursuit of the team's objectives.

Celebrating successes, both big and small, is an integral part of maintaining team morale and motivation. Acknowledging achievements reinforces the value of each member's contributions and strengthens the team's resolve to tackle future challenges. Celebrations need not be grandiose; even simple gestures of appreciation can have a profound impact on team spirit. These moments of recognition serve as reminders of what the team has accomplished together and inspire continued collaboration and effort.

Inclusivity and diversity are vital components of a thriving team. Embracing diverse perspectives enriches the team's problem-solving capabilities and fosters creativity and innovation. An inclusive environment ensures that all members feel valued and

respected, regardless of their background or identity.
This sense of belonging encourages individuals to
bring their authentic selves to the team, enhancing
collaboration and driving success.

The social connections formed within a team extend
beyond professional interactions. These bonds create
a support network that can be relied upon in times of
need, both personally and professionally. Strong
social connections contribute to a positive team
culture, where members feel a sense of camaraderie
and mutual support. This culture not only enhances
team performance but also contributes to individual
well-being and job satisfaction.

Roles and Responsibilities Finding Your Place

In the intricate tapestry of teamwork, understanding
and defining roles and responsibilities is akin to
setting the stage for a successful performance. Each
team member, much like an actor in a play, must
know their part, their cues, and how they fit into the
larger narrative. This clarity not only ensures smooth
collaboration but also empowers individuals to
contribute their best, fostering a sense of purpose and
belonging within the team.

The first step in finding one's place within a team is
recognizing the unique skills and strengths each
member brings to the table. This involves a thorough
assessment of individual capabilities, experiences, and
preferences. By identifying these attributes, teams can
assign roles that align with each member's strengths,

maximizing efficiency and productivity. For instance, a team member with a knack for detail-oriented tasks might excel in roles that require meticulous planning and execution, while someone with strong interpersonal skills might thrive in roles that involve client interactions or team coordination.

Once roles are defined, it is crucial to communicate them clearly to all team members. This transparency eliminates ambiguity and ensures that everyone understands their responsibilities and how they contribute to the team's objectives. Clear communication also helps prevent overlaps and gaps in responsibilities, which can lead to confusion and inefficiencies. Regular team meetings and updates can serve as platforms for discussing roles, addressing any concerns, and making necessary adjustments as the project evolves.

Flexibility is another key aspect of defining roles and responsibilities. While it is important to have clearly defined roles, it is equally important to remain adaptable to changing circumstances and team dynamics. Projects often encounter unforeseen challenges that require team members to step outside their usual roles and take on additional responsibilities. Encouraging a culture of flexibility and cross-functional collaboration can help teams navigate these challenges effectively, ensuring that the project stays on track even in the face of adversity.

In addition to defining roles, it is essential to establish accountability within the team. Accountability ensures that each member takes ownership of their tasks and is committed to delivering results. This can be achieved by setting clear expectations, establishing deadlines, and regularly reviewing progress. Accountability not only drives performance but also fosters a sense of trust and reliability among team members, as everyone knows they can depend on each other to fulfill their commitments.

Finding one's place within a team also involves understanding the interdependencies between different roles. Team members must recognize how their work impacts others and how they can support each other to achieve common goals. This interconnectedness requires effective communication and collaboration, as well as a willingness to offer assistance and seek help when needed. By fostering a culture of mutual support, teams can create an environment where everyone feels valued and motivated to contribute their best.

Leadership plays a pivotal role in defining and managing roles and responsibilities within a team. Effective leaders possess the ability to identify individual strengths, delegate tasks appropriately, and provide guidance and support to team members. They also serve as role models, demonstrating the importance of accountability, flexibility, and collaboration. By fostering an inclusive and supportive environment, leaders can empower team members to take ownership of their roles and contribute to the team's success.

It is important to recognize that roles and responsibilities are not static; they evolve as the team grows and the project progresses. Regularly revisiting and reassessing roles can help teams adapt to changing needs and ensure that everyone remains aligned with the team's objectives. This ongoing evaluation also provides opportunities for team members to develop new skills, take on new challenges, and expand their contributions to the team.

In the journey of finding one's place within a team, self-awareness and reflection are invaluable tools. Team members should take the time to reflect on their strengths, weaknesses, and areas for growth. By understanding their own capabilities and limitations, individuals can seek out roles that align with their skills and interests, while also identifying opportunities for personal and professional development.

Communication The Lifeline of Effective Teams

Communication is the heartbeat of any successful team, the vital force that keeps it alive and thriving. It is the channel through which ideas are exchanged, plans are formulated, and relationships are nurtured. Without effective communication, even the most talented teams can falter, as misunderstandings and misalignments create barriers to success. Understanding the nuances of communication within a team setting is essential for fostering collaboration, building trust, and achieving shared goals.

At the core of effective team communication is the ability to listen actively. Active listening involves more than just hearing words; it requires paying attention to the speaker's message, interpreting their intent, and responding thoughtfully. This level of engagement demonstrates respect and empathy, encouraging open dialogue and mutual understanding. When team members feel heard and valued, they are more likely to contribute their ideas and perspectives, enriching the team's collective knowledge and creativity.

Clear and concise communication is equally important. In a team environment, where multiple voices and viewpoints converge, clarity is key to ensuring that messages are understood and acted upon. This involves articulating thoughts in a straightforward manner, avoiding jargon or ambiguous language that could lead to confusion. It also means being mindful of the audience, tailoring the message to suit the needs and preferences of different team members. By prioritizing clarity, teams can minimize misunderstandings and streamline decision-making processes.

Nonverbal communication plays a significant role in team interactions as well. Body language, facial expressions, and tone of voice can convey emotions and attitudes that words alone may not capture. Being attuned to these nonverbal cues can enhance understanding and foster stronger connections between team members. For instance, maintaining eye contact and using open gestures can signal attentiveness and openness, while a warm tone can convey encouragement and support. By being aware of and responsive to nonverbal signals, teams can create a more inclusive and supportive communication environment.

Feedback is a crucial component of effective team communication. Constructive feedback provides valuable insights into performance and areas for improvement, helping team members grow and develop their skills. However, delivering feedback requires sensitivity and tact. It should be specific, focused on behaviors rather than personal attributes, and delivered in a manner that encourages positive change. Equally important is the ability to receive feedback with an open mind, viewing it as an opportunity for growth rather than criticism. By fostering a culture of constructive feedback, teams can continuously improve and adapt to changing circumstances.

Technology has transformed the way teams communicate, offering a plethora of tools and platforms that facilitate collaboration across distances and time zones. From instant messaging and video conferencing to collaborative document editing and project management software, these tools enable seamless communication and coordination. However, the abundance of communication channels can also lead to information overload and fragmentation. To mitigate this, teams should establish clear guidelines for using different communication tools, ensuring that information is shared efficiently and effectively.

Cultural differences can also impact team communication, particularly in diverse or global teams. Language barriers, varying communication styles, and differing cultural norms can create challenges in understanding and collaboration. To navigate these differences, teams should cultivate cultural awareness and sensitivity, recognizing and respecting the diverse backgrounds and perspectives of team members. This involves being open to learning about and adapting to different communication styles, as well as fostering an inclusive environment where all voices are heard and valued.

Conflict is an inevitable aspect of team dynamics, and effective communication is key to resolving disagreements and maintaining harmony. When conflicts arise, it is important to address them promptly and constructively, focusing on finding solutions rather than assigning blame. This requires open and honest communication, where team members feel comfortable expressing their concerns and working together to reach a resolution. By approaching conflicts with a collaborative mindset, teams can turn potential obstacles into opportunities for growth and innovation.

Trust is the foundation of effective team communication. When team members trust each other, they are more likely to share information, collaborate openly, and support one another. Building trust requires consistency, transparency, and integrity in communication. It involves being honest about challenges and limitations, keeping commitments, and demonstrating reliability. By fostering a culture of trust, teams can create a safe space where communication flows freely and collaboration thrives.

Trust Building The Foundation of Success

Trust is the bedrock upon which successful teams are built, a vital element that underpins every interaction and decision. It is the invisible glue that binds team members together, fostering an environment where collaboration can flourish and innovation can thrive. Without trust, even the most talented teams can struggle to achieve their full potential, as doubt and uncertainty create barriers to effective communication and cooperation.

Building trust within a team begins with transparency. Open and honest communication is essential for establishing trust, as it demonstrates integrity and reliability. Team members must feel confident that they are receiving accurate information and that their contributions are valued. This requires leaders and team members alike to be forthcoming about challenges, successes, and any changes that may impact the team. By fostering a culture of transparency, teams can create a foundation of trust that encourages open dialogue and mutual respect.

Consistency is another key component of trust-building. When team members consistently follow through on their commitments and deliver on their promises, they demonstrate reliability and dependability. This consistency reassures team members that they can rely on each other to fulfill their roles and responsibilities, creating a sense of stability and predictability within the team. It is important for team members to set realistic expectations and to communicate any potential obstacles that may impact their ability to meet deadlines or deliver results. By managing expectations and maintaining consistency, teams can strengthen the trust that underpins their collaboration.

Empathy plays a crucial role in building trust within a team. By demonstrating understanding and compassion for each other's perspectives and experiences, team members can create a supportive and inclusive environment where everyone feels valued and respected. Empathy involves actively listening to others, acknowledging their feelings, and responding with kindness and consideration. When team members feel understood and supported, they are more likely to trust their colleagues and to engage in open and honest communication.

Accountability is essential for maintaining trust within a team. Each member must take responsibility for their actions and be willing to own up to mistakes or shortcomings. This accountability fosters a culture of trust, as team members know that they can rely on each other to be honest and transparent about their performance. It is important for leaders to model accountability by acknowledging their own mistakes and demonstrating a commitment to continuous improvement. By fostering a culture of accountability, teams can build trust and create an environment where everyone feels empowered to take risks and innovate.

Trust is also built through shared experiences and collaboration. When team members work together to overcome challenges and achieve common goals, they develop a sense of camaraderie and mutual respect. These shared experiences create a bond that strengthens trust and reinforces the team's commitment to each other. Team-building activities and collaborative projects can provide opportunities for team members to connect on a personal level and to build trust through shared accomplishments.

Conflict resolution is an important aspect of trust-building within a team. Conflicts are inevitable in any team setting, but how they are managed can significantly impact trust. It is important for teams to address conflicts promptly and constructively, focusing on finding solutions rather than assigning blame. By approaching conflicts with an open mind and a willingness to listen, teams can turn potential obstacles into opportunities for growth and innovation. Effective conflict resolution demonstrates a commitment to collaboration and reinforces trust within the team.

Trust is not a one-time achievement but an ongoing process that requires continuous effort and attention. Teams must regularly assess and nurture the trust within their group, addressing any issues or concerns that may arise. This involves creating opportunities for open dialogue, providing feedback, and celebrating successes together. By prioritizing trust-building activities and maintaining a focus on transparency, consistency, empathy, and accountability, teams can create a strong foundation for success.

In the journey of building trust, leadership plays a pivotal role. Leaders set the tone for the team's culture and are instrumental in fostering an environment where trust can thrive. Effective leaders demonstrate integrity, communicate openly, and model the behaviors they wish to see in their team members. They create a safe space where team members feel comfortable expressing their ideas and concerns, and they provide support and guidance to help the team navigate challenges. By embodying the principles of trust-building, leaders can inspire their teams to achieve remarkable success.

Conflict Resolution Turning Disagreements into Opportunities

Conflict is an inevitable part of any team dynamic, arising from the diverse perspectives, experiences, and personalities that each member brings to the table. While disagreements can sometimes lead to tension and disruption, they also present valuable opportunities for growth, innovation, and strengthened relationships. The key to harnessing the potential of conflict lies in effective resolution strategies that transform discord into constructive dialogue and collaborative problem-solving.

Understanding the root causes of conflict is the first step in addressing it effectively. Conflicts often stem from miscommunication, differing values or goals, competition for resources, or personality clashes. By identifying the underlying issues, teams can address the core problems rather than merely treating the symptoms. This requires open and honest communication, where team members feel comfortable expressing their concerns and perspectives without fear of judgment or retaliation.

Active listening is a crucial skill in conflict resolution. It involves fully engaging with the speaker, seeking to understand their viewpoint, and acknowledging their feelings. By demonstrating empathy and respect, team members can create an environment where everyone feels heard and valued. This not only helps to de-escalate tensions but also fosters a sense of trust and collaboration. Active listening also involves asking clarifying questions and paraphrasing the speaker's message to ensure accurate understanding and to demonstrate genuine interest in resolving the conflict.

Once the root causes of the conflict have been identified, it is important to explore potential solutions collaboratively. This involves brainstorming and evaluating different options, considering the needs and interests of all parties involved. Encouraging creativity and open-mindedness can lead to innovative solutions that address the concerns of all team members. It is important to focus on finding win-win outcomes, where everyone feels that their needs have been met and that the resolution is fair and equitable.

Effective conflict resolution also requires a willingness to compromise. In many cases, team members may need to make concessions to reach a mutually acceptable solution. This involves prioritizing the team's goals over individual preferences and being open to alternative approaches. By demonstrating flexibility and a commitment to the team's success, team members can build stronger relationships and foster a culture of collaboration.

Mediation can be a valuable tool in resolving conflicts that are particularly complex or emotionally charged. A neutral third party, such as a team leader or an external mediator, can facilitate discussions and help guide the team toward a resolution. The mediator's role is to ensure that all voices are heard, to keep the conversation focused on finding solutions, and to help the team navigate any impasses. Mediation can provide a structured framework for resolving conflicts and can help to maintain a positive and productive team environment.

It is important to recognize that conflict resolution is not a one-time event but an ongoing process. Teams should regularly reflect on their conflict resolution strategies and assess their effectiveness. This involves seeking feedback from team members, identifying areas for improvement, and making necessary adjustments. By continuously refining their approach to conflict resolution, teams can enhance their ability to navigate disagreements and turn them into opportunities for growth and innovation.

Leadership plays a critical role in fostering a culture of constructive conflict resolution. Effective leaders model the behaviors they wish to see in their team members, demonstrating active listening, empathy, and a commitment to collaboration. They create a safe space where team members feel comfortable expressing their concerns and where conflicts are addressed promptly and constructively. By setting clear expectations and providing guidance and support, leaders can empower their teams to resolve conflicts effectively and to harness the potential of disagreements for positive change.

In addition to resolving conflicts as they arise, teams can take proactive steps to prevent conflicts from escalating. This involves establishing clear communication channels, setting expectations for behavior and performance, and fostering a culture of respect and inclusivity. By creating an environment where team members feel valued and supported, teams can reduce the likelihood of conflicts and create a more harmonious and productive team dynamic.

Chapter 2

The Psychology of Teamwork

Motivation and Morale Keeping the Team Spirit Alive

Motivation and morale are the lifeblood of any team, the driving forces that propel individuals to push beyond their limits and achieve collective success. When team spirit is high, challenges become opportunities, and obstacles are met with resilience and creativity. However, maintaining motivation and morale requires intentional effort and a deep understanding of the factors that influence team dynamics. By nurturing these elements, teams can create an environment where enthusiasm and commitment thrive.

At the heart of motivation lies a sense of purpose. Team members need to understand the significance of their work and how it contributes to the larger goals of the organization. This sense of purpose can be cultivated by clearly communicating the team's vision and objectives, ensuring that everyone understands their role in achieving them. When individuals see the impact of their contributions, they are more likely to feel motivated and engaged. Leaders play a crucial role in reinforcing this sense of purpose by regularly highlighting the team's achievements and progress toward their goals.

Recognition and appreciation are powerful motivators that can significantly boost team morale.

Acknowledging the efforts and accomplishments of team members not only reinforces their value but also fosters a culture of positivity and encouragement. Recognition can take many forms, from public praise during team meetings to personalized notes of appreciation. The key is to ensure that recognition is genuine and specific, highlighting the unique contributions of each individual. By celebrating successes, both big and small, teams can create an environment where members feel valued and motivated to continue striving for excellence.

Autonomy and empowerment are also critical components of motivation. When team members are given the freedom to make decisions and take ownership of their work, they are more likely to feel invested in the team's success. Empowering individuals to contribute their ideas and solutions fosters a sense of ownership and accountability, driving motivation and innovation. Leaders can support autonomy by providing clear guidelines and expectations while allowing team members the flexibility to determine how best to achieve their objectives.

A supportive and inclusive team culture is essential for maintaining high morale. Team members need to feel that they are part of a cohesive unit where their voices are heard and respected. This involves fostering open communication, encouraging collaboration, and creating a safe space where individuals can express their ideas and concerns without fear of judgment. Inclusivity also means recognizing and valuing the diverse perspectives and experiences that each team member brings to the table. By embracing diversity and promoting a culture of respect and inclusion, teams can create an environment where everyone feels a sense of belonging and motivation.

Opportunities for growth and development are important motivators that can enhance team morale. When individuals have the chance to learn new skills, take on new challenges, and advance their careers, they are more likely to feel motivated and engaged. Providing access to training, mentorship, and career development opportunities can help team members reach their full potential and contribute more effectively to the team's success. Leaders can support growth by identifying and nurturing the strengths of each team member and providing opportunities for them to expand their skills and responsibilities.

Work-life balance is a critical factor in maintaining motivation and morale. When team members feel overwhelmed or burned out, their motivation and productivity can suffer. It is important for teams to recognize the importance of balance and to support each other in achieving it. This may involve setting realistic expectations, encouraging breaks and time off, and promoting a culture of flexibility and understanding. By prioritizing well-being and balance, teams can create an environment where members feel energized and motivated to contribute their best.

Team-building activities can also play a significant role in boosting morale and motivation. These activities provide opportunities for team members to connect on a personal level, build trust, and strengthen relationships. Whether it's a team retreat, a group outing, or a simple team lunch, these shared experiences can foster camaraderie and a sense of unity. By investing in team-building activities, teams can create a positive and supportive environment where motivation and morale flourish.

Leadership is instrumental in maintaining motivation and morale within a team. Effective leaders inspire and motivate their teams by setting a positive example, providing guidance and support, and fostering a culture of trust and collaboration. They are attuned to the needs and concerns of their team members and are proactive in addressing any issues that may impact motivation and morale. By demonstrating empathy, integrity, and a commitment to the team's success, leaders can inspire their teams to achieve remarkable results.

Emotional Intelligence Navigating Team Emotions

Emotional intelligence (EI) is the compass that guides teams through the complex landscape of emotions, enabling them to navigate interpersonal dynamics with grace and understanding. It is the ability to recognize, understand, and manage one's own emotions, as well as the emotions of others. In a team setting, where diverse personalities and perspectives converge, emotional intelligence is a critical skill that fosters collaboration, enhances communication, and strengthens relationships.

At the core of emotional intelligence is self-awareness. This involves recognizing and understanding one's own emotions, as well as the impact they have on thoughts and behaviors. Self-aware team members are better equipped to manage their emotions, preventing them from negatively affecting their interactions with others. They are also more attuned to their strengths and weaknesses, allowing them to contribute more effectively to the team's goals. Developing self-awareness requires reflection and introspection, as well as a willingness to seek feedback from others.

Self-regulation is another key component of emotional intelligence. It involves the ability to control and manage one's emotions, particularly in challenging or stressful situations. Team members who can regulate their emotions are less likely to react impulsively or defensively, allowing them to respond to conflicts and challenges with composure and thoughtfulness. Self-regulation also involves adaptability, the ability to adjust one's approach and behavior in response to changing circumstances. By cultivating self-regulation, teams can create a more stable and harmonious environment where collaboration can thrive.

Empathy is a cornerstone of emotional intelligence, enabling team members to understand and relate to the emotions of others. Empathetic individuals are able to put themselves in others' shoes, recognizing and validating their feelings and perspectives. This fosters a sense of connection and trust, as team members feel understood and supported. Empathy also enhances communication, as it encourages active listening and open dialogue. By prioritizing empathy, teams can create an inclusive and supportive culture where everyone feels valued and respected.

Social skills are an essential aspect of emotional intelligence, encompassing the ability to build and maintain positive relationships with others. This involves effective communication, collaboration, and conflict resolution skills, as well as the ability to inspire and motivate others. Team members with strong social skills are able to navigate interpersonal dynamics with ease, fostering a sense of camaraderie and teamwork. They are also adept at managing conflicts and facilitating constructive dialogue, turning potential obstacles into opportunities for growth and innovation.

Motivation, another component of emotional intelligence, drives individuals to pursue their goals with passion and perseverance. Motivated team members are committed to the team's success and are willing to put in the effort required to achieve their objectives. They are also resilient in the face of setbacks, viewing challenges as opportunities for learning and development. By fostering a culture of motivation, teams can create an environment where individuals are inspired to contribute their best and to support each other in achieving their shared goals.

Developing emotional intelligence within a team requires intentional effort and practice. It involves creating opportunities for team members to enhance their self-awareness, self-regulation, empathy, social skills, and motivation. This can be achieved through training and development programs, as well as through regular feedback and reflection. Leaders play a crucial role in fostering emotional intelligence by modeling emotionally intelligent behaviors and by creating a safe space where team members feel comfortable expressing their emotions and seeking support.

In addition to individual development, teams can enhance their collective emotional intelligence by fostering a culture of openness and trust. This involves encouraging open communication, where team members feel comfortable sharing their thoughts and feelings without fear of judgment or retaliation. It also involves promoting a culture of respect and inclusivity, where diverse perspectives and experiences are valued and celebrated. By creating an environment where emotional intelligence is prioritized, teams can enhance their ability to navigate the complexities of teamwork and to achieve their shared goals.

Emotional intelligence is not a static trait but a dynamic skill that can be developed and strengthened over time. Teams should regularly assess their emotional intelligence and identify areas for improvement. This involves seeking feedback from team members, reflecting on past experiences, and setting goals for personal and collective development. By continuously enhancing their emotional intelligence, teams can create a more positive and productive environment where collaboration and innovation can thrive.

The Power of Positive Reinforcement

Positive reinforcement is a powerful tool that can transform team dynamics, enhance performance, and foster a culture of growth and collaboration. By recognizing and rewarding desired behaviors, positive reinforcement encourages individuals to continue exhibiting those behaviors, creating a ripple effect that benefits the entire team. Understanding how to effectively implement positive reinforcement can lead to increased motivation, improved morale, and a more cohesive team environment.

At its core, positive reinforcement involves acknowledging and rewarding behaviors that contribute to the team's success. This can take many forms, from verbal praise and recognition to tangible rewards such as bonuses or promotions. The key is to ensure that the reinforcement is meaningful and aligned with the individual's values and motivations. For some, a simple "thank you" or public acknowledgment may be sufficient, while others may be motivated by more tangible rewards. By tailoring reinforcement to the individual, teams can maximize its impact and effectiveness.

Timing is crucial when it comes to positive reinforcement. To be effective, reinforcement should be delivered as soon as possible after the desired behavior occurs. This helps to create a clear connection between the behavior and the reward, reinforcing the association in the individual's mind. Delayed reinforcement can weaken this connection and reduce its effectiveness. By providing timely reinforcement, teams can encourage the repetition of positive behaviors and create a culture of continuous improvement.

Consistency is another important factor in the successful implementation of positive reinforcement.

Reinforcement should be applied consistently across the team, ensuring that all members are recognized and rewarded for their contributions. Inconsistent reinforcement can lead to perceptions of favoritism or unfairness, which can undermine morale and motivation. By applying reinforcement consistently, teams can create a sense of equity and fairness, fostering a positive and inclusive team culture.

Specificity is key when providing positive reinforcement. General praise, such as "good job," may not be as effective as specific feedback that highlights the particular behavior or achievement being recognized. For example, acknowledging a team member's attention to detail in a project report or their ability to collaborate effectively with others provides clear and actionable feedback. This specificity not only reinforces the desired behavior but also provides guidance for future performance.

Positive reinforcement can also be used to encourage teamwork and collaboration. By recognizing and rewarding behaviors that contribute to the team's collective success, such as effective communication, problem-solving, or support for colleagues, teams can foster a culture of collaboration and mutual support. This can be achieved through team-based rewards, such as group celebrations or shared incentives, which reinforce the importance of working together toward common goals.

Leaders play a critical role in modeling and promoting positive reinforcement within a team. By demonstrating a commitment to recognizing and rewarding positive behaviors, leaders set the tone for the team's culture and encourage others to do the same. This involves being attentive to the contributions of team members, providing regular feedback, and celebrating successes both big and small. Leaders can also empower team members to recognize and reinforce each other's positive behaviors, creating a culture of peer support and encouragement.

In addition to formal recognition and rewards, informal positive reinforcement can be equally impactful. Simple gestures, such as a smile, a nod of approval, or a personal note of thanks, can convey appreciation and reinforce positive behaviors. These informal reinforcements can be integrated into daily interactions, creating a culture of positivity and encouragement that permeates the team environment.

While positive reinforcement is a powerful tool, it is important to balance it with constructive feedback and accountability. Reinforcement should not be used to overlook or excuse poor performance or undesirable behaviors. Instead, it should be part of a broader performance management strategy that includes regular feedback, goal setting, and opportunities for growth and development. By balancing positive reinforcement with constructive feedback, teams can create an environment where individuals feel supported and motivated to achieve their best.

The impact of positive reinforcement extends beyond individual performance to influence the overall team dynamic. By fostering a culture of recognition and appreciation, teams can enhance morale, increase engagement, and reduce turnover. Team members who feel valued and appreciated are more likely to be committed to the team's success and to contribute their best efforts. This creates a positive feedback loop, where motivated and engaged team members drive the team's success, leading to further recognition and reinforcement.

Overcoming Psychological Barriers

Psychological barriers can be formidable obstacles in the path to personal and professional success. These barriers, often rooted in fear, self-doubt, and limiting beliefs, can hinder individuals from reaching their full potential and achieving their goals. However, by identifying and addressing these barriers, individuals can unlock new opportunities for growth and transformation. Understanding the nature of psychological barriers and developing strategies to overcome them is essential for anyone seeking to thrive in a competitive and ever-changing world.

Fear is one of the most common psychological barriers that individuals face. Whether it's fear of failure, fear of rejection, or fear of the unknown, these anxieties can paralyze decision-making and stifle creativity. To overcome fear, it's important to confront it head-on and to reframe it as an opportunity for growth. This involves acknowledging the fear, understanding its origins, and challenging the assumptions that underlie it. By taking small, manageable steps toward the source of fear, individuals can gradually build confidence and resilience, transforming fear into a catalyst for positive change.

Self-doubt is another pervasive psychological barrier that can undermine confidence and motivation. It often manifests as an inner critic, questioning one's abilities and worthiness. To combat self-doubt, individuals must cultivate self-compassion and recognize their inherent value. This involves challenging negative self-talk and replacing it with affirmations of strength and capability. By focusing on past successes and the unique strengths they bring to the table, individuals can build a more positive self-image and develop the confidence needed to pursue their goals.

Limiting beliefs are deeply ingrained assumptions that can restrict one's potential and limit opportunities. These beliefs often stem from past experiences, societal expectations, or cultural norms, and they can manifest as thoughts such as "I'm not good enough" or "I can't do this." To overcome limiting beliefs, individuals must first identify and challenge them. This involves examining the evidence for and against these beliefs and considering alternative perspectives. By reframing limiting beliefs as opportunities for growth and learning, individuals can expand their horizons and embrace new possibilities.

Procrastination is a common psychological barrier that can impede progress and productivity. It often arises from a fear of failure or a lack of motivation, leading individuals to delay tasks and avoid responsibilities. To overcome procrastination, it's important to break tasks into smaller, manageable steps and to set clear, achievable goals. By creating a structured plan and establishing deadlines, individuals can increase accountability and motivation. Additionally, identifying and addressing the underlying causes of procrastination, such as perfectionism or fear of judgment, can help individuals develop more effective strategies for managing their time and responsibilities.

Perfectionism is another psychological barrier that can hinder progress and stifle creativity. The pursuit of perfection can lead to unrealistic expectations and a fear of making mistakes, preventing individuals from taking risks and trying new things. To overcome perfectionism, it's important to embrace the concept of "good enough" and to recognize that mistakes are a natural part of the learning process. By focusing on progress rather than perfection, individuals can cultivate a growth mindset and develop the resilience needed to navigate challenges and setbacks.

Imposter syndrome is a psychological barrier that affects many high-achieving individuals, leading them to doubt their accomplishments and fear being exposed as a fraud. This syndrome can undermine confidence and motivation, preventing individuals from fully embracing their success. To combat imposter syndrome, it's important to acknowledge and celebrate one's achievements and to recognize the hard work and dedication that contributed to them. Seeking support from mentors, peers, or a therapist can also provide valuable perspective and encouragement, helping individuals build confidence and self-assurance.

Social anxiety is a psychological barrier that can impact interpersonal relationships and professional opportunities. It often involves a fear of judgment or rejection, leading individuals to avoid social interactions and networking opportunities. To overcome social anxiety, it's important to gradually expose oneself to social situations and to practice effective communication skills. By focusing on building genuine connections and finding common ground with others, individuals can develop the confidence needed to navigate social interactions and expand their professional network.

Mindfulness and self-awareness are powerful tools for overcoming psychological barriers. By cultivating a greater awareness of one's thoughts, emotions, and behaviors, individuals can identify and address the barriers that hold them back. Mindfulness practices, such as meditation or journaling, can help individuals develop a deeper understanding of their inner world and build resilience in the face of challenges. By fostering a sense of presence and acceptance, individuals can navigate psychological barriers with greater ease and confidence.

Support from others is also crucial in overcoming psychological barriers. Whether it's seeking guidance from a mentor, sharing experiences with peers, or working with a therapist, external support can provide valuable perspective and encouragement. By building a strong support network, individuals can gain the confidence and motivation needed to tackle their barriers and pursue their goals.

The Role of Leadership in Team Psychology

Leadership is the cornerstone of team psychology, shaping the environment in which individuals collaborate, innovate, and achieve shared goals. The influence of a leader extends beyond mere task management; it permeates the emotional and psychological fabric of the team. Effective leadership fosters a culture of trust, motivation, and resilience, enabling teams to navigate challenges and seize opportunities with confidence and cohesion.

A leader's vision is a powerful motivator that aligns the team with a common purpose. By clearly articulating the team's goals and the path to achieving them, leaders provide direction and inspiration. This vision serves as a guiding light, helping team members understand the significance of their contributions and how they fit into the larger picture. When individuals see the impact of their work, they are more likely to feel motivated and engaged, driving the team toward success.

Communication is a fundamental aspect of leadership that directly impacts team psychology. Open and transparent communication fosters trust and collaboration, creating an environment where team members feel comfortable sharing their ideas and concerns. Leaders who actively listen and encourage dialogue demonstrate respect and empathy, strengthening the bonds within the team. By facilitating effective communication, leaders can ensure that everyone is on the same page and that potential conflicts are addressed constructively.

Emotional intelligence is a critical trait for leaders, enabling them to navigate the complexities of team dynamics with sensitivity and insight. Leaders with high emotional intelligence are attuned to the emotions of their team members and can respond with empathy and understanding. This ability to connect on an emotional level fosters a sense of belonging and support, enhancing team morale and cohesion. By modeling emotional intelligence, leaders set the tone for a positive and inclusive team culture.

Empowerment is a key strategy for leaders seeking to enhance team psychology. By delegating authority and encouraging autonomy, leaders demonstrate trust in their team members' abilities. This empowerment fosters a sense of ownership and accountability, motivating individuals to take initiative and contribute their best efforts. Leaders can support empowerment by providing the necessary resources and guidance while allowing team members the freedom to explore and innovate.

Recognition and appreciation are powerful tools for leaders to boost team morale and motivation. Acknowledging the efforts and achievements of team members reinforces their value and encourages continued excellence. Leaders can express appreciation through verbal praise, public recognition, or tangible rewards, ensuring that the reinforcement is meaningful and aligned with individual motivations. By celebrating successes, leaders create a culture of positivity and encouragement that permeates the team environment.

Adaptability is an essential quality for leaders in today's fast-paced and ever-changing world. The ability to pivot and respond to new challenges and opportunities is crucial for maintaining team momentum and resilience. Leaders who embrace change and encourage flexibility within their teams foster a culture of innovation and continuous improvement. By modeling adaptability, leaders inspire their teams to embrace change with confidence and creativity.

Conflict resolution is a vital skill for leaders, as conflicts are inevitable in any team setting. Effective leaders address conflicts promptly and constructively, facilitating open dialogue and seeking win-win solutions. By creating a safe space for team members to express their concerns and perspectives, leaders can transform conflicts into opportunities for growth and collaboration. This proactive approach to conflict resolution strengthens team relationships and enhances overall team psychology.

Mentorship and development are integral components of leadership that contribute to a thriving team environment. Leaders who invest in the growth and development of their team members demonstrate a commitment to their success and well-being. By providing opportunities for learning, skill-building, and career advancement, leaders empower individuals to reach their full potential. This investment in development not only enhances individual performance but also contributes to the team's collective success.

Resilience is a quality that leaders must cultivate within themselves and their teams. The ability to persevere in the face of adversity and to bounce back from setbacks is crucial for long-term success. Leaders can foster resilience by modeling a positive attitude, encouraging a growth mindset, and providing support during challenging times. By building a resilient team, leaders ensure that their team can navigate the ups and downs of the journey with strength and determination.

Chapter 3

Building Stronger Bonds

Creating a Shared Vision and Goals

A shared vision and clearly defined goals are the foundation upon which successful teams are built. They provide direction, purpose, and a sense of unity, aligning individual efforts toward a common objective. Crafting a shared vision and setting goals that resonate with every team member requires thoughtful consideration and collaborative effort. When done effectively, this process can transform a group of individuals into a cohesive and motivated team, ready to tackle challenges and achieve remarkable outcomes.

The journey toward creating a shared vision begins with understanding the core values and aspirations of the team. These values serve as guiding principles, shaping the team's identity and influencing its decisions and actions. Engaging team members in discussions about their personal values and how they align with the team's mission can foster a sense of ownership and commitment. By identifying common values, teams can create a vision that reflects their collective aspirations and inspires them to work together toward a shared future.

A compelling vision is both aspirational and achievable, striking a balance between ambition and realism. It paints a vivid picture of the future, capturing the imagination and enthusiasm of the team. To craft such a vision, leaders must engage team members in a collaborative process, encouraging them to share their ideas and perspectives. This inclusive approach ensures that the vision resonates with everyone and reflects the diverse strengths and experiences of the team. By involving team members in the visioning process, leaders can foster a sense of ownership and commitment, motivating individuals to contribute their best efforts toward achieving the vision.

Once a shared vision is established, the next step is to translate it into actionable goals. These goals serve as milestones on the journey toward the vision, providing clear and measurable targets for the team to strive toward. Effective goal-setting involves breaking down the vision into specific, achievable objectives that align with the team's capabilities and resources. This process requires careful planning and consideration, ensuring that goals are realistic, time-bound, and aligned with the team's overall strategy.

SMART goals—specific, measurable, achievable, relevant, and time-bound—are a widely used framework for effective goal-setting. By ensuring that goals meet these criteria, teams can create a clear roadmap for success, with defined metrics for tracking progress and evaluating performance. Specific goals provide clarity and focus, while measurable goals enable teams to assess their progress and make data-driven decisions. Achievable goals ensure that the team remains motivated and confident, while relevant goals align with the team's vision and priorities. Time-bound goals create a sense of urgency and accountability, driving the team to take action and achieve results.

Communication is a critical component of the goal-setting process, ensuring that all team members understand and are aligned with the goals. Leaders must clearly articulate the goals and the rationale behind them, providing context and clarity for the team. Regular communication and updates on progress help to maintain momentum and motivation, reinforcing the team's commitment to achieving the goals. By fostering open dialogue and encouraging feedback, leaders can ensure that the goals remain relevant and responsive to the team's evolving needs and circumstances.

Collaboration is essential for achieving shared goals, as it leverages the diverse strengths and expertise of the team. By fostering a culture of collaboration, teams can harness the collective creativity and problem-solving abilities of their members, driving innovation and success. This involves creating opportunities for team members to work together, share ideas, and support each other in achieving their objectives. Leaders can facilitate collaboration by providing the necessary resources and tools, as well as by creating an environment that encourages open communication and mutual respect.

Accountability is a key factor in the successful achievement of goals, ensuring that team members take responsibility for their contributions and actions. By establishing clear roles and responsibilities, teams can create a sense of ownership and accountability, motivating individuals to deliver on their commitments. Regular check-ins and progress reviews provide opportunities for team members to assess their performance, identify areas for improvement, and celebrate successes. By fostering a culture of accountability, teams can ensure that everyone remains focused and committed to achieving the shared goals.

Flexibility is also important in the goal-setting process, as it allows teams to adapt to changing circumstances and seize new opportunities. While goals provide direction and focus, they should not be rigid or inflexible. Teams must be willing to reassess and adjust their goals as needed, responding to new information and challenges. This requires a willingness to embrace change and to view setbacks as opportunities for learning and growth. By maintaining a flexible and adaptive approach, teams can remain resilient and responsive, navigating the complexities of their environment with confidence and agility.

Celebrating achievements and milestones is an important aspect of maintaining motivation and morale as teams work toward their goals. Recognizing and rewarding progress reinforces the value of the team's efforts and encourages continued commitment. Celebrations can take many forms, from formal recognition ceremonies to informal team gatherings, and should be tailored to the preferences and values of the team. By acknowledging successes and expressing appreciation, teams can create a positive and supportive environment that fosters motivation and engagement.

Team-Building Activities Beyond the Office

Team-building activities that extend beyond the confines of the office can invigorate a team, fostering stronger bonds and enhancing collaboration in ways that traditional workplace interactions often cannot. These activities provide a refreshing change of scenery, allowing team members to connect on a personal level and discover new facets of each other's personalities. By stepping outside the usual work environment, teams can break down barriers, build trust, and cultivate a sense of camaraderie that translates into improved performance and morale back at the office.

Outdoor adventures offer a dynamic way to engage team members and encourage collaboration. Activities such as hiking, kayaking, or rock climbing challenge individuals to step out of their comfort zones and rely on each other for support and guidance. These experiences promote teamwork and communication, as participants must work together to navigate obstacles and achieve common goals. The shared sense of accomplishment that comes from conquering a physical challenge can strengthen team bonds and boost confidence, creating a lasting impact on team dynamics.

Community service projects provide an opportunity for teams to give back to their communities while fostering a sense of purpose and unity. Volunteering at a local food bank, participating in a neighborhood clean-up, or organizing a charity event allows team members to work together toward a meaningful cause.

These activities not only enhance team cohesion but also instill a sense of pride and fulfillment, as individuals see the positive impact of their collective efforts. By engaging in community service, teams can develop a deeper appreciation for each other's strengths and contributions, fostering a culture of empathy and collaboration.

Creative workshops offer a platform for team members to express themselves and explore new skills in a relaxed and supportive environment. Whether it's a painting class, a cooking workshop, or a music jam session, these activities encourage creativity and innovation, allowing individuals to tap into their artistic potential. By engaging in creative pursuits, team members can break free from routine thinking patterns and discover new ways of problem-solving and collaboration. These workshops also provide an opportunity for team members to share their talents and interests, fostering a sense of connection and mutual respect.

Cultural experiences, such as attending a theater performance, visiting a museum, or exploring a local festival, can broaden team members' perspectives and inspire new ideas. These activities expose individuals to diverse cultures and viewpoints, encouraging open-mindedness and curiosity. By experiencing art, history, and culture together, teams can engage in meaningful discussions and reflections, deepening their understanding of each other and the world around them. Cultural experiences can also spark creativity and innovation, as team members draw inspiration from the richness and diversity of human expression.

Team-building retreats offer an immersive experience that allows teams to focus on personal and professional development in a serene and distraction-free setting. These retreats often combine workshops, outdoor activities, and relaxation, providing a holistic approach to team-building. By stepping away from the daily grind, team members can reflect on their goals, strengthen their relationships, and recharge their energy. Retreats also provide an opportunity for teams to set intentions and align their vision, fostering a sense of unity and purpose that carries over into their work.

Escape rooms and problem-solving challenges offer a fun and engaging way for teams to test their collaboration and communication skills. These activities require participants to work together to solve puzzles and overcome obstacles, promoting critical thinking and teamwork. The pressure of a time limit adds an element of excitement and urgency, encouraging team members to think on their feet and rely on each other's strengths. Successfully completing a challenge can boost team morale and confidence, reinforcing the value of collaboration and effective communication.

Sports and recreational activities provide a lively and energetic way for teams to bond and have fun together. Whether it's a friendly game of soccer, a bowling night, or a yoga class, these activities promote physical fitness and well-being while fostering a sense of camaraderie. Participating in sports encourages healthy competition and teamwork, as individuals must coordinate their efforts and support each other to achieve success. Recreational activities also provide an opportunity for team members to relax and unwind, strengthening their relationships and enhancing their overall well-being.

Cooking challenges and culinary experiences offer a delicious way for teams to collaborate and connect. Whether it's a team cook-off, a baking class, or a wine-tasting event, these activities encourage creativity and teamwork in a fun and interactive setting. Cooking together requires communication and coordination, as team members must work together to prepare a meal or complete a culinary challenge. Sharing a meal fosters a sense of community and celebration, as individuals come together to enjoy the fruits of their labor and appreciate each other's contributions.

Celebrating Successes Big and Small

Celebrating successes, whether monumental or modest, is a vital practice that can significantly enhance team morale, motivation, and cohesion. Recognizing achievements not only reinforces positive behaviors but also fosters a culture of appreciation and encouragement. By acknowledging both the grand milestones and the smaller victories, teams can cultivate an environment where every contribution is valued, and every effort is acknowledged.

The power of celebration lies in its ability to create a sense of accomplishment and pride among team members. When individuals see their hard work and dedication being recognized, it validates their efforts and reinforces their commitment to the team's goals.

This recognition can take many forms, from formal awards and ceremonies to informal gestures of appreciation. The key is to ensure that the celebration is meaningful and resonates with the team, reflecting their values and culture.

Celebrating big successes, such as the completion of a major project or the achievement of a significant milestone, provides an opportunity for the team to come together and reflect on their collective accomplishments. These celebrations can be grand events, such as a company-wide party or a team outing, where everyone can relax and enjoy the fruits of their labor. By marking these occasions with memorable experiences, teams can strengthen their bonds and create lasting memories that reinforce their sense of unity and purpose.

However, it's equally important to recognize the smaller successes that occur along the way. These might include meeting a challenging deadline, resolving a complex issue, or simply making progress toward a long-term goal. Celebrating these incremental achievements helps to maintain momentum and motivation, reminding team members that their efforts are making a difference. Simple gestures, such as a heartfelt thank-you note, a shout-out in a team meeting, or a small token of appreciation, can go a long way in acknowledging these contributions and boosting morale.

The act of celebration also provides an opportunity for reflection and learning. By taking the time to acknowledge what went well and what contributed to the success, teams can identify best practices and strategies that can be applied to future projects. This reflection can also highlight areas for improvement, encouraging a culture of continuous learning and growth. By celebrating successes, teams can reinforce the behaviors and practices that lead to positive outcomes, creating a cycle of success and improvement.

Incorporating celebrations into the team's routine can also enhance engagement and retention. When team members feel valued and appreciated, they are more likely to be committed to the team's success and to remain with the organization. Celebrations create a positive and supportive work environment, where individuals feel connected to their colleagues and motivated to contribute their best efforts. This sense of belonging and purpose can lead to increased job satisfaction and reduced turnover, benefiting both the team and the organization as a whole.

Leaders play a crucial role in fostering a culture of celebration within their teams. By modeling appreciation and recognition, leaders set the tone for the team's culture and encourage others to do the same. This involves being attentive to the contributions of team members, providing regular feedback, and celebrating successes both big and small. Leaders can also empower team members to recognize and celebrate each other's achievements, creating a culture of peer support and encouragement.

It's important to tailor celebrations to the preferences and values of the team. What resonates with one team may not be meaningful to another, so it's essential to understand what motivates and inspires team members. This might involve soliciting input from the team on how they would like to celebrate their successes or experimenting with different approaches to see what works best. By personalizing celebrations, teams can ensure that they are meaningful and impactful, reinforcing the team's culture and values.

Celebrations can also be an opportunity to strengthen relationships and build camaraderie within the team. By coming together to celebrate, team members can connect on a personal level, share experiences, and build trust. These social interactions can enhance team dynamics and create a sense of community, where individuals feel supported and valued. By fostering strong relationships, teams can improve communication, collaboration, and overall performance.

In addition to traditional celebrations, teams can explore creative and unique ways to recognize achievements. This might include creating a "wall of fame" to showcase team accomplishments, organizing a team-building activity to celebrate a milestone, or even starting a tradition of sharing success stories during team meetings. These creative approaches can add an element of fun and excitement to the celebration, making it a memorable and enjoyable experience for everyone involved.

Fostering Inclusivity and Diversity

Inclusivity and diversity are not just buzzwords; they are essential components of a thriving and innovative team environment. Embracing these principles means recognizing and valuing the unique perspectives, experiences, and talents that each individual brings to the table. By fostering an inclusive and diverse team, organizations can unlock a wealth of creativity, drive innovation, and enhance overall performance. The journey toward inclusivity and diversity requires intentional effort, open-mindedness, and a commitment to creating a culture where everyone feels valued and empowered to contribute.

The first step in fostering inclusivity and diversity is to cultivate an environment of respect and openness. This involves actively listening to team members, acknowledging their perspectives, and creating a safe space for dialogue and expression. Leaders play a crucial role in setting the tone for inclusivity by modeling respectful behavior and encouraging open communication. By demonstrating a genuine interest in understanding and appreciating diverse viewpoints, leaders can inspire team members to do the same, fostering a culture of mutual respect and collaboration.

Recruitment and hiring practices are critical in building a diverse team. Organizations must be intentional in seeking out candidates from a wide range of backgrounds, experiences, and skill sets. This involves expanding recruitment efforts to reach underrepresented groups and removing biases from the hiring process. By prioritizing diversity in recruitment, organizations can ensure that they are attracting a broad spectrum of talent, enriching the team's capabilities and perspectives.

Once a diverse team is in place, it's important to ensure that all members feel included and valued. This means recognizing and addressing any barriers to participation and engagement, such as language differences, cultural misunderstandings, or unconscious biases. Providing resources and support, such as language training or cultural competency workshops, can help team members navigate these challenges and feel more comfortable and confident in their roles. By actively addressing barriers to inclusion, organizations can create an environment where everyone feels empowered to contribute their best efforts.

Mentorship and sponsorship programs can be powerful tools for fostering inclusivity and diversity. By pairing team members with mentors or sponsors who can provide guidance, support, and advocacy, organizations can help individuals navigate their career paths and achieve their goals. These programs can be particularly beneficial for individuals from underrepresented groups, providing them with the resources and networks needed to succeed. By investing in mentorship and sponsorship, organizations can demonstrate their commitment to supporting the growth and development of all team members.

Training and education are essential components of fostering inclusivity and diversity. Providing team members with opportunities to learn about different cultures, perspectives, and experiences can enhance their understanding and appreciation of diversity. This might involve workshops, seminars, or online courses that cover topics such as cultural competency, unconscious bias, or inclusive leadership. By equipping team members with the knowledge and skills needed to navigate a diverse environment, organizations can create a more inclusive and harmonious team culture.

Celebrating diversity is another important aspect of fostering inclusivity. This involves recognizing and honoring the unique contributions and achievements of team members from diverse backgrounds. Celebrations can take many forms, from cultural events and festivals to recognition awards and spotlights on individual achievements. By celebrating diversity, organizations can create a sense of pride and belonging among team members, reinforcing the value of inclusivity and diversity.

Feedback and continuous improvement are key to sustaining an inclusive and diverse team culture. Organizations must be open to feedback from team members and willing to make changes to enhance inclusivity and diversity. This might involve conducting regular surveys or focus groups to gather input on the team's culture and identifying areas for improvement. By actively seeking feedback and making data-driven decisions, organizations can ensure that they are continuously evolving and adapting to meet the needs of their diverse team.

Leadership commitment is crucial in fostering inclusivity and diversity. Leaders must be vocal advocates for these principles, demonstrating their commitment through their actions and decisions. This involves setting clear goals and metrics for diversity and inclusion, holding themselves and others accountable for progress, and allocating resources to support initiatives. By prioritizing inclusivity and diversity, leaders can inspire their teams to do the same, creating a culture where everyone feels valued and empowered.

The benefits of fostering inclusivity and diversity extend beyond the team to the organization as a whole. Diverse teams are more innovative, as they bring a wide range of perspectives and ideas to the table. This diversity of thought can lead to more creative solutions and better decision-making, driving organizational success. Additionally, organizations that prioritize inclusivity and diversity are more attractive to top talent, as they demonstrate a commitment to creating a supportive and empowering work environment.

The Impact of Social Connections on Team Performance

Social connections within a team are the invisible threads that weave individuals into a cohesive unit, significantly influencing team performance and overall success. These connections foster trust, collaboration, and a sense of belonging, creating an environment where team members feel motivated and empowered to contribute their best efforts. Understanding the impact of social connections on team performance is crucial for leaders and organizations seeking to enhance productivity, innovation, and morale.

At the heart of effective social connections is trust. When team members trust one another, they are more likely to communicate openly, share ideas, and collaborate effectively. Trust reduces the fear of judgment or criticism, allowing individuals to express themselves freely and take risks. This openness fosters a culture of innovation, where diverse perspectives are valued and new ideas are encouraged. Trust also enhances accountability, as team members feel a sense of responsibility to each other and to the team's goals. By building trust, teams can create a strong foundation for collaboration and success.

Communication is another critical aspect of social connections that impacts team performance. Effective communication ensures that team members are aligned with the team's objectives, understand their roles and responsibilities, and are aware of any challenges or changes. Social connections facilitate informal communication, allowing team members to share information and insights in a more relaxed and spontaneous manner. This informal exchange of ideas can lead to creative problem-solving and innovation, as team members build on each other's thoughts and experiences. By fostering open and transparent communication, teams can enhance collaboration and drive performance.

A sense of belonging is essential for team members to feel connected and engaged. When individuals feel that they are part of a supportive and inclusive team, they are more likely to be motivated and committed to the team's success. Social connections create a sense of community, where team members feel valued and appreciated for their contributions. This sense of belonging enhances morale and job satisfaction, reducing turnover and increasing retention. By cultivating a culture of inclusion and support, teams can create an environment where everyone feels empowered to contribute their best efforts.

Collaboration is at the core of team performance, and social connections play a vital role in facilitating effective collaboration. When team members have strong social connections, they are more likely to work together harmoniously, leveraging each other's strengths and expertise. These connections enable individuals to coordinate their efforts, share resources, and support each other in achieving common goals. Collaboration also fosters a sense of shared ownership and accountability, as team members work together to overcome challenges and achieve success. By strengthening social connections, teams can enhance collaboration and drive performance.

Social connections also contribute to resilience, enabling teams to navigate challenges and setbacks with confidence and determination. When team members have strong social bonds, they are more likely to support each other during difficult times, providing encouragement and assistance. This support fosters a sense of resilience, as individuals feel empowered to persevere and overcome obstacles. Resilient teams are better equipped to adapt to change, seize opportunities, and achieve long-term success. By fostering social connections, teams can build resilience and enhance their ability to thrive in a dynamic and competitive environment.

Leaders play a crucial role in fostering social connections within their teams. By modeling open communication, trust, and collaboration, leaders set the tone for the team's culture and encourage others to do the same. Leaders can also create opportunities for team members to connect and build relationships, such as team-building activities, social events, or informal gatherings. By prioritizing social connections, leaders can enhance team performance and create a positive and supportive work environment.

It's important to recognize that social connections are not one-size-fits-all; they must be tailored to the unique needs and preferences of the team. Some team members may prefer structured interactions, while others may thrive in more informal settings. Understanding these preferences and creating opportunities for diverse types of interactions can enhance social connections and ensure that everyone feels included and valued. By personalizing social connections, teams can create a more cohesive and harmonious environment.

Technology can also play a role in facilitating social connections, especially in remote or distributed teams. Virtual communication tools, such as video conferencing, instant messaging, and collaboration platforms, can help bridge the gap and enable team members to connect and collaborate effectively. These tools provide opportunities for informal interactions, such as virtual coffee breaks or team chats, allowing team members to build relationships and strengthen social connections. By leveraging technology, teams can enhance social connections and drive performance, even in a virtual environment.

Chapter 4

Strategies for Effective Collaboration

Collaborative Tools and Technologies

In today's fast-paced and interconnected world, collaborative tools and technologies have become indispensable for teams striving to achieve their goals efficiently and effectively. These tools facilitate communication, streamline workflows, and enhance productivity, enabling teams to collaborate seamlessly regardless of geographical boundaries. Understanding the landscape of collaborative technologies and how to leverage them can significantly impact a team's success, fostering innovation and driving performance.

The evolution of collaborative tools has transformed the way teams work, breaking down traditional barriers and enabling real-time communication and collaboration. From project management platforms to instant messaging apps, these tools offer a wide range of functionalities designed to meet the diverse needs of modern teams. Selecting the right tools requires a thoughtful assessment of the team's objectives, workflows, and preferences, ensuring that the chosen technologies align with the team's goals and enhance their ability to collaborate effectively.

Project management platforms are a cornerstone of collaborative technologies, providing teams with a centralized hub for planning, tracking, and managing their work. These platforms offer features such as task assignment, progress tracking, and deadline management, enabling teams to stay organized and focused on their objectives. By providing visibility into the team's workload and progress, project management tools facilitate accountability and transparency, ensuring that everyone is aligned and working toward the same goals. Popular platforms like Trello, Asana, and Monday.com offer customizable features that can be tailored to the specific needs of the team, enhancing their ability to collaborate and succeed.

Communication tools are another essential component of collaborative technologies, enabling teams to connect and communicate in real-time. Instant messaging apps, such as Slack and Microsoft Teams, provide a platform for quick and informal communication, allowing team members to share information, ask questions, and collaborate on tasks. These tools also offer features such as file sharing, video conferencing, and integration with other applications, enhancing their functionality and versatility. By facilitating seamless communication, these tools help teams stay connected and engaged, fostering a sense of community and collaboration.

Document collaboration tools, such as Google Workspace and Microsoft Office 365, enable teams to work together on documents, spreadsheets, and presentations in real-time. These tools offer features such as version control, commenting, and simultaneous editing, allowing team members to collaborate efficiently and effectively. By providing a platform for real-time collaboration, these tools enhance productivity and creativity, enabling teams to produce high-quality work and achieve their goals. The ability to access and edit documents from anywhere also provides flexibility and convenience, supporting remote and distributed teams in their efforts to collaborate and succeed.

Cloud storage solutions, such as Dropbox and OneDrive, offer teams a secure and accessible platform for storing and sharing files. These tools provide features such as file synchronization, access control, and backup, ensuring that team members can access the information they need when they need it. By providing a centralized repository for files and documents, cloud storage solutions enhance collaboration and efficiency, enabling teams to work together seamlessly and effectively. The ability to access files from any device also supports remote work and flexibility, empowering teams to collaborate and succeed in a dynamic and fast-paced environment.

Video conferencing tools, such as Zoom and Google Meet, have become essential for teams working remotely or across different locations. These tools provide a platform for face-to-face communication, enabling teams to connect and collaborate in real-time. Video conferencing tools offer features such as screen sharing, recording, and breakout rooms, enhancing their functionality and versatility. By facilitating virtual meetings and discussions, these tools help teams stay connected and engaged, fostering a sense of community and collaboration. The ability to connect with team members from anywhere also provides flexibility and convenience, supporting remote and distributed teams in their efforts to collaborate and succeed.

Integration and automation tools, such as Zapier and IFTTT, enable teams to streamline their workflows and enhance productivity. These tools provide a platform for connecting different applications and automating repetitive tasks, reducing the need for manual intervention and enhancing efficiency. By automating routine processes, teams can focus on more strategic and value-added activities, driving performance and success. The ability to integrate different tools and applications also enhances collaboration and connectivity, enabling teams to work together seamlessly and effectively.

Security and privacy are critical considerations when selecting and implementing collaborative tools and technologies. Teams must ensure that their chosen tools comply with relevant regulations and standards, protecting sensitive information and maintaining confidentiality. This involves assessing the security features and protocols of each tool, such as encryption, access control, and data protection, and implementing best practices for security and privacy. By prioritizing security and privacy, teams can protect their information and maintain trust, enabling them to collaborate and succeed with confidence.

Training and support are essential for ensuring that team members can effectively use and leverage collaborative tools and technologies. Providing training and resources, such as tutorials, workshops, and user guides, can help team members develop the skills and knowledge needed to use these tools effectively. Ongoing support, such as help desks and technical assistance, can also ensure that team members have access to the resources and assistance they need to overcome challenges and succeed. By investing in training and support, teams can enhance their ability to collaborate and achieve their goals.

Decision-Making Processes Achieving Consensus

Decision-making is a fundamental aspect of any team's success, and achieving consensus is often the key to making effective and sustainable decisions. Consensus decision-making involves finding a solution that everyone can support, even if it is not their first choice. This approach fosters collaboration, inclusivity, and commitment, ensuring that all team members feel heard and valued. By understanding and implementing effective decision-making processes, teams can enhance their ability to achieve consensus and drive success.

The journey to consensus begins with creating an environment where open communication and active listening are prioritized. Team members must feel comfortable expressing their opinions, concerns, and ideas without fear of judgment or retribution. This requires a culture of respect and trust, where diverse perspectives are valued and encouraged. Leaders play a crucial role in setting the tone for open communication by modeling active listening and encouraging team members to share their thoughts. By fostering an environment of openness and respect, teams can lay the foundation for effective consensus-building.

Clearly defining the problem or decision at hand is a critical step in the decision-making process. Teams must ensure that everyone has a shared understanding of the issue and the desired outcome. This involves gathering relevant information, identifying key stakeholders, and clarifying the criteria for a successful decision. By establishing a common understanding, teams can align their efforts and focus on finding a solution that meets the needs of all stakeholders.

Brainstorming is a valuable tool for generating a wide range of ideas and solutions. During this phase, team members are encouraged to think creatively and propose diverse options without judgment or criticism. The goal is to generate as many ideas as possible, fostering a sense of innovation and collaboration. By encouraging creativity and open-mindedness, teams can explore a variety of possibilities and identify potential solutions that may not have been considered otherwise.

Once a range of options has been generated, teams must evaluate each option based on the established criteria. This involves assessing the pros and cons of each solution, considering the potential impact on stakeholders, and identifying any potential risks or challenges. By conducting a thorough evaluation, teams can narrow down the options and focus on the most viable solutions. This phase requires critical thinking and analytical skills, as team members must weigh the benefits and drawbacks of each option and consider the long-term implications.

Facilitating discussion and debate is an essential part of the consensus-building process. Team members must have the opportunity to express their opinions, ask questions, and challenge assumptions. This dialogue allows for a deeper understanding of the options and encourages team members to consider different perspectives. By engaging in constructive debate, teams can identify common ground and work toward a solution that meets the needs of all stakeholders. It is important to ensure that discussions remain respectful and focused on the issue at hand, avoiding personal attacks or defensiveness.

Reaching consensus often requires compromise and flexibility. Team members must be willing to adjust their positions and consider alternative solutions in order to achieve a decision that everyone can support. This may involve finding a middle ground or integrating elements from multiple options to create a hybrid solution. By demonstrating a willingness to compromise, team members can build trust and strengthen their commitment to the final decision.

Once consensus has been reached, it is important to document the decision and communicate it to all stakeholders. This ensures that everyone is aware of the outcome and understands their roles and responsibilities moving forward. Clear communication also reinforces accountability and transparency, ensuring that the decision is implemented effectively and efficiently. By documenting and communicating the decision, teams can ensure that everyone is aligned and committed to the agreed-upon solution.

Reflecting on the decision-making process is a valuable opportunity for learning and improvement. Teams should take the time to evaluate what worked well and what could be improved in future decision-making efforts. This reflection can highlight best practices and identify areas for growth, fostering a culture of continuous learning and development. By learning from past experiences, teams can enhance their decision-making processes and improve their ability to achieve consensus in the future.

Achieving consensus in decision-making is not always easy, and it may not be possible in every situation. There may be times when a decision must be made quickly, or when consensus cannot be reached despite best efforts. In these cases, it is important for leaders to make a decision that aligns with the team's goals and values, while ensuring that all perspectives have been considered. By balancing the need for consensus with the need for timely and effective decision-making, teams can navigate challenges and achieve success.

Balancing Individual and Team Goals

Balancing individual and team goals is a delicate dance that requires careful consideration and strategic alignment. In any organization, individuals bring their unique aspirations, skills, and motivations to the table, while teams work collectively toward shared objectives. The challenge lies in harmonizing these personal ambitions with the broader goals of the team, ensuring that both are met without compromising one for the other. Achieving this balance is crucial for fostering a motivated, cohesive, and high-performing team.

The first step in balancing individual and team goals is to establish a clear understanding of both sets of objectives. Team leaders must communicate the team's goals and vision effectively, ensuring that every member understands the purpose and direction of their collective efforts. This clarity provides a framework within which individual goals can be aligned. Simultaneously, leaders should encourage team members to articulate their personal goals, aspirations, and areas of interest. By understanding what drives each individual, leaders can identify synergies and potential conflicts between personal and team objectives.

Once both individual and team goals are clearly defined, the next step is to identify areas of alignment and potential integration. This involves looking for opportunities where individual aspirations can contribute to the team's success. For example, if a team member is passionate about developing a particular skill, leaders can assign them tasks or projects that allow them to hone that skill while advancing the team's objectives. By aligning individual strengths and interests with team needs, organizations can create a win-win situation where personal growth and team success go hand in hand.

Regular communication and feedback are essential for maintaining the balance between individual and team goals. Leaders should engage in ongoing dialogue with team members, providing feedback on their performance and progress toward both personal and team objectives. This feedback loop allows individuals to adjust their efforts and priorities as needed, ensuring that they remain aligned with the team's goals. It also provides an opportunity for leaders to recognize and celebrate individual contributions, reinforcing the value of each team member's efforts.

Flexibility is a key component of balancing individual and team goals. Organizations must be willing to adapt and adjust their strategies to accommodate the evolving needs and aspirations of their team members. This might involve revisiting and revising goals, reallocating resources, or providing additional support and training. By demonstrating flexibility and responsiveness, organizations can create an environment where individuals feel valued and empowered to pursue their personal goals while contributing to the team's success.

Empowerment and autonomy are also critical factors in achieving this balance. When team members are given the autonomy to pursue their personal goals within the context of the team's objectives, they are more likely to feel motivated and engaged. Empowering individuals to take ownership of their work and make decisions fosters a sense of responsibility and accountability, driving both personal and team success. Leaders can support this empowerment by providing the necessary resources, guidance, and support, while also encouraging innovation and creativity.

Recognition and reward systems play a significant role in balancing individual and team goals. Organizations should implement systems that acknowledge and reward both individual achievements and team successes. This might involve offering incentives for reaching personal milestones, as well as celebrating collective accomplishments. By recognizing and rewarding both individual and team efforts, organizations can reinforce the importance of balancing personal and collective goals, motivating team members to strive for excellence in both areas.

Mentorship and coaching can also support the balance between individual and team goals. By pairing team members with mentors or coaches, organizations can provide guidance and support for personal development while ensuring alignment with team objectives. Mentors can help individuals identify opportunities for growth, navigate challenges, and develop strategies for achieving their goals. This support fosters a culture of continuous learning and development, enhancing both individual and team performance.

It's important to recognize that balancing individual and team goals is an ongoing process that requires continuous attention and adjustment. As team members grow and evolve, their personal goals may change, necessitating a reevaluation of their alignment with team objectives. Organizations must remain vigilant and proactive in addressing these changes, ensuring that both individual and team goals remain aligned and mutually supportive.

Encouraging Creativity and Innovation

Creativity and innovation are the lifeblood of any successful team, driving progress and enabling organizations to adapt and thrive in an ever-changing world. Encouraging these qualities within a team requires more than just a desire for new ideas; it demands a deliberate and supportive environment where creativity can flourish and innovation can take root. By fostering a culture that values experimentation, embraces diverse perspectives, and encourages risk-taking, teams can unlock their full creative potential and achieve remarkable outcomes.

Creating a culture that encourages creativity begins with establishing an environment where team members feel safe to express their ideas without fear of judgment or criticism. Psychological safety is a crucial component of this environment, as it allows individuals to take risks, share unconventional ideas, and challenge the status quo. Leaders play a pivotal role in cultivating psychological safety by modeling openness, encouraging diverse viewpoints, and demonstrating a willingness to learn from failure. By fostering a supportive and inclusive atmosphere, teams can create a fertile ground for creativity and innovation to thrive.

Diverse perspectives are a powerful catalyst for creativity, as they bring a wide range of experiences, ideas, and approaches to the table. Encouraging diversity within a team involves actively seeking out and valuing different backgrounds, skills, and viewpoints. This diversity can be achieved through inclusive hiring practices, cross-functional collaboration, and creating opportunities for team members to share their unique insights. By embracing diversity, teams can enhance their creative potential and generate innovative solutions that reflect a broader range of perspectives.

Encouraging experimentation and risk-taking is essential for fostering innovation. Teams must be willing to explore new ideas, test hypotheses, and learn from both successes and failures. This requires a shift in mindset from viewing failure as a setback to seeing it as an opportunity for growth and learning. Leaders can support this mindset by celebrating experimentation, recognizing the value of learning from mistakes, and providing the resources and support needed to explore new ideas. By creating a culture that values experimentation, teams can unlock their creative potential and drive innovation.

Providing time and space for creativity is another important aspect of encouraging innovation. Teams need dedicated time to brainstorm, explore new ideas, and engage in creative thinking. This might involve setting aside regular time for brainstorming sessions, creating spaces that inspire creativity, or encouraging team members to pursue passion projects. By prioritizing time and space for creativity, teams can ensure that innovation is an integral part of their work, rather than an afterthought.

Collaboration is a key driver of creativity and innovation, as it allows team members to build on each other's ideas and leverage their collective strengths. Encouraging collaboration involves creating opportunities for team members to work together, share ideas, and co-create solutions. This might involve cross-functional projects, collaborative workshops, or informal brainstorming sessions. By fostering a culture of collaboration, teams can enhance their creative potential and generate innovative solutions that reflect the collective wisdom of the group.

Recognition and reward systems play a significant role in encouraging creativity and innovation. By acknowledging and celebrating creative efforts and innovative solutions, organizations can reinforce the value of these qualities and motivate team members to continue pursuing new ideas. This recognition can take many forms, from formal awards and incentives to informal praise and acknowledgment. By recognizing and rewarding creativity, teams can create a culture that values and encourages innovation.

Leadership support is crucial for fostering creativity and innovation within a team. Leaders must demonstrate a commitment to these qualities by providing the resources, support, and guidance needed to explore new ideas and pursue innovative solutions. This might involve investing in training and development, providing access to new technologies, or creating opportunities for team members to learn from industry experts. By prioritizing creativity and innovation, leaders can inspire their teams to do the same, driving progress and achieving remarkable outcomes.

Continuous learning and development are essential for maintaining a culture of creativity and innovation. Teams must be committed to ongoing learning, seeking out new knowledge, skills, and perspectives that can enhance their creative potential. This might involve attending workshops, conferences, or training sessions, as well as encouraging team members to pursue their own learning and development goals. By fostering a culture of continuous learning, teams can stay at the forefront of innovation and drive long-term success.

Managing Remote Teams Challenges and Solutions

Managing remote teams presents a unique set of challenges and opportunities that require thoughtful strategies and solutions. As organizations increasingly embrace remote work, leaders must navigate the complexities of managing teams that are dispersed across different locations and time zones. By understanding the challenges associated with remote work and implementing effective solutions, leaders can foster a productive and engaged remote team that achieves its goals.

One of the primary challenges of managing remote teams is maintaining effective communication. In a remote setting, team members may feel isolated or disconnected from their colleagues, leading to misunderstandings and miscommunications. To address this challenge, leaders must prioritize clear and consistent communication, utilizing a variety of tools and platforms to keep team members connected. Regular video meetings, instant messaging, and collaborative platforms can facilitate real-time communication and ensure that everyone is aligned and informed. By fostering open and transparent communication, leaders can bridge the gap and create a sense of connection and community within the remote team.

Building trust and rapport among remote team members is another critical challenge. In a traditional office setting, team members have the opportunity to build relationships through face-to-face interactions and informal conversations. In a remote environment, these opportunities are limited, making it more difficult to establish trust and camaraderie. To overcome this challenge, leaders can create opportunities for team members to connect on a personal level, such as virtual team-building activities, informal coffee chats, or online social events. By fostering a sense of belonging and connection, leaders can build trust and rapport within the remote team, enhancing collaboration and engagement.

Managing productivity and performance in a remote setting requires a shift in focus from hours worked to outcomes achieved. In a remote environment, team members have greater flexibility in how and when they work, which can lead to variations in productivity and performance. To address this challenge, leaders must set clear expectations and goals, providing team members with the autonomy to manage their own work while holding them accountable for results. Regular check-ins and performance reviews can help ensure that team members are meeting their objectives and provide an opportunity for feedback and support. By focusing on outcomes rather than hours, leaders can empower remote team members to take ownership of their work and achieve their goals.

Ensuring access to the necessary tools and resources is essential for remote team success. In a remote setting, team members rely on technology to communicate, collaborate, and complete their work. Leaders must ensure that team members have access to the tools and resources they need to be productive and successful. This may involve providing access to software and applications, offering technical support, or investing in training and development. By equipping remote team members with the necessary tools and resources, leaders can enhance productivity and performance.

Maintaining work-life balance is a common challenge for remote team members, as the boundaries between work and personal life can become blurred. In a remote setting, team members may feel pressure to be constantly available or struggle to disconnect from work. To address this challenge, leaders can encourage team members to establish clear boundaries and routines, such as setting specific work hours, taking regular breaks, and creating a dedicated workspace. By promoting work-life balance, leaders can support the well-being and mental health of remote team members, enhancing their engagement and productivity.

Cultural differences and time zone challenges can also impact remote team dynamics. In a global remote team, team members may come from diverse cultural backgrounds and work in different time zones, leading to potential misunderstandings and scheduling conflicts. To address these challenges, leaders must foster a culture of inclusivity and respect, encouraging team members to embrace diversity and learn from each other's perspectives. Flexible scheduling and asynchronous communication can help accommodate different time zones and ensure that all team members can participate and contribute. By embracing diversity and flexibility, leaders can create a cohesive and harmonious remote team.

Providing support and development opportunities is crucial for remote team success. In a remote setting, team members may feel disconnected from the organization's culture and opportunities for growth. Leaders must prioritize professional development and career advancement, offering remote team members access to training, mentorship, and networking opportunities. Regular feedback and coaching can also support remote team members in their development and help them achieve their career goals. By investing in the growth and development of remote team members, leaders can enhance engagement and retention.

Chapter 5

Achieving Victory Together

Setting and Achieving Team Milestones

Setting and achieving team milestones is a critical component of successful project management and team collaboration. Milestones serve as key markers of progress, helping teams to stay on track and maintain momentum toward their ultimate goals. By establishing clear and achievable milestones, teams can break down complex projects into manageable segments, ensuring that each step is completed efficiently and effectively. This chapter delves into the strategies and practices that can help teams set and achieve meaningful milestones, fostering a sense of accomplishment and driving success.

The process of setting team milestones begins with a clear understanding of the project's overall objectives and desired outcomes. Teams must have a shared vision of what they aim to achieve, as this provides the foundation for identifying the key milestones that will guide their progress. This involves breaking down the project into smaller, actionable tasks and determining the critical points at which progress can be measured. By establishing a roadmap of milestones, teams can create a structured plan that outlines the path to success.

Once the overarching goals are defined, the next step is to prioritize and sequence the milestones. Not all milestones are created equal, and some may hold more significance or urgency than others. Teams must assess the relative importance of each milestone and determine the logical order in which they should be achieved. This prioritization helps to allocate resources effectively and ensures that the team focuses on the most critical tasks first. By sequencing milestones strategically, teams can maintain a steady pace and avoid bottlenecks or delays.

Setting realistic and achievable milestones is essential for maintaining team motivation and engagement. Milestones should be challenging enough to inspire effort and commitment, yet attainable within the given timeframe and resources. Teams must consider factors such as available skills, time constraints, and potential obstacles when defining their milestones. By setting realistic targets, teams can build confidence and momentum as they achieve each milestone, reinforcing their commitment to the project's success.

Clear communication is vital when setting and achieving team milestones. All team members must understand the significance of each milestone, their roles and responsibilities, and the criteria for success. This involves regular updates and discussions to ensure that everyone is aligned and informed. By fostering open communication, teams can address any challenges or concerns that arise, ensuring that milestones are met on time and to the required standard.

Monitoring progress and performance is a crucial aspect of achieving team milestones. Teams must establish mechanisms for tracking their progress and evaluating their performance against the defined milestones. This might involve regular check-ins, progress reports, or performance metrics that provide visibility into the team's achievements. By monitoring progress, teams can identify any deviations from the plan and take corrective action as needed, ensuring that they remain on track to achieve their goals.

Celebrating the achievement of milestones is an important practice that reinforces team motivation and morale. Recognizing and acknowledging the hard work and dedication that went into reaching a milestone fosters a sense of accomplishment and pride. Celebrations can take many forms, from formal recognition and rewards to informal gatherings or team outings. By celebrating milestones, teams can strengthen their sense of camaraderie and commitment, motivating them to continue striving for success.

Flexibility and adaptability are key qualities for teams working toward milestones. Projects rarely go exactly as planned, and teams must be prepared to adjust their strategies and timelines in response to changing circumstances. This might involve revisiting and revising milestones, reallocating resources, or exploring alternative solutions. By remaining flexible and adaptable, teams can navigate challenges and setbacks, ensuring that they continue to make progress toward their goals.

Continuous improvement is an integral part of setting and achieving team milestones. Teams should take the time to reflect on their performance and identify areas for growth and development. This might involve conducting post-milestone reviews, gathering feedback from team members, or analyzing performance data. By learning from their experiences, teams can enhance their processes and practices, improving their ability to set and achieve milestones in the future.

Measuring Team Performance and Success

Measuring team performance and success is a multifaceted endeavor that requires a blend of quantitative metrics and qualitative insights. Understanding how well a team is performing involves more than just looking at the end results; it requires a comprehensive evaluation of processes, collaboration, and individual contributions. By employing a balanced approach to measurement, teams can gain valuable insights into their strengths and areas for improvement, ultimately driving enhanced performance and success.

The foundation of measuring team performance lies in establishing clear and measurable objectives. These objectives should align with the team's overall goals and provide a benchmark against which progress can be assessed. By defining specific, measurable, achievable, relevant, and time-bound (SMART) goals, teams can create a framework for evaluating their performance. This clarity ensures that all team members understand what is expected of them and how their contributions impact the team's success.

Quantitative metrics are a crucial component of performance measurement, providing objective data that can be analyzed and compared over time. These metrics might include key performance indicators (KPIs) such as productivity rates, project completion times, error rates, or customer satisfaction scores. By tracking these metrics, teams can identify trends, assess their efficiency, and pinpoint areas where improvements are needed. However, it's important to select metrics that are meaningful and relevant to the team's objectives, avoiding the temptation to measure everything simply because it can be measured.

While quantitative metrics provide valuable data, they do not capture the full picture of team performance. Qualitative insights are equally important, offering a deeper understanding of the dynamics and processes that contribute to success. Gathering qualitative feedback from team members, stakeholders, and customers can provide insights into areas such as communication, collaboration, and innovation. This feedback can be collected through surveys, interviews, or focus groups, allowing teams to explore the underlying factors that influence their performance.

Regular performance reviews and assessments are essential for maintaining accountability and driving continuous improvement. These reviews provide an opportunity for team members to reflect on their achievements, discuss challenges, and set goals for the future. By conducting regular assessments, teams can ensure that they remain aligned with their objectives and make necessary adjustments to their strategies and processes. Performance reviews also foster a culture of transparency and open communication, encouraging team members to share their perspectives and contribute to the team's growth.

Collaboration and teamwork are critical components of team performance, and measuring these aspects requires a focus on both individual and collective contributions. Evaluating how well team members work together, share information, and support each other can provide insights into the team's overall effectiveness. This might involve assessing factors such as communication skills, conflict resolution, and the ability to leverage diverse perspectives. By understanding the dynamics of collaboration, teams can identify areas for improvement and implement strategies to enhance their teamwork.

Innovation and creativity are also important indicators of team success, reflecting the team's ability to adapt and thrive in a changing environment. Measuring innovation involves assessing the team's capacity to generate new ideas, experiment with different approaches, and implement creative solutions. This might include tracking the number of new initiatives launched, the impact of innovative projects, or the team's ability to learn from failures. By fostering a culture of innovation, teams can drive continuous improvement and achieve long-term success.

Recognition and reward systems play a significant role in reinforcing positive performance and motivating team members to excel. By acknowledging and celebrating individual and team achievements, organizations can reinforce the behaviors and practices that contribute to success. This recognition can take many forms, from formal awards and incentives to informal praise and acknowledgment. By recognizing and rewarding performance, teams can create a culture of excellence and inspire team members to strive for their best.

Continuous learning and development are essential for sustaining high performance and achieving success. Teams must be committed to ongoing learning, seeking out new knowledge, skills, and perspectives that can enhance their performance. This might involve attending workshops, conferences, or training sessions, as well as encouraging team members to pursue their own learning and development goals. By fostering a culture of continuous learning, teams can stay at the forefront of their field and drive long-term success.

Learning from Failures A Path to Improvement

Failure, often perceived as a setback, can be a powerful catalyst for growth and improvement. In the realm of team dynamics and project management, learning from failures is an essential practice that can lead to innovation, resilience, and long-term success. By embracing failure as an opportunity for learning, teams can transform challenges into valuable lessons, fostering a culture of continuous improvement and adaptability.

The first step in learning from failures is to cultivate a mindset that views failure as a natural and valuable part of the learning process. This involves shifting the perception of failure from a negative outcome to a stepping stone toward success. Leaders play a crucial role in fostering this mindset by encouraging openness, curiosity, and a willingness to take risks. By creating an environment where team members feel safe to experiment and fail, leaders can unlock the potential for creativity and innovation.

Analyzing failures is a critical component of the learning process. When a project or initiative does not go as planned, teams must take the time to reflect on what went wrong and why. This involves conducting a thorough analysis of the factors that contributed to the failure, including both internal and external influences. By examining the root causes of failure, teams can gain insights into the underlying issues and identify areas for improvement. This analysis should be approached with an open mind and a focus on learning, rather than assigning blame.

Once the root causes of failure have been identified, the next step is to develop actionable strategies for improvement. This involves translating the lessons learned from failure into concrete actions that can enhance future performance. Teams should collaborate to brainstorm potential solutions, evaluate their feasibility, and prioritize the most promising options. By developing a clear plan for improvement, teams can turn failure into a valuable learning experience that drives progress and success.

Communication is a vital aspect of learning from failures. Teams must engage in open and honest discussions about their experiences, sharing insights and perspectives that can inform future efforts. This involves creating a culture of transparency and trust, where team members feel comfortable discussing their failures and learning from each other. By fostering open communication, teams can leverage the collective wisdom of their members, enhancing their ability to learn and grow.

Resilience is a key quality that enables teams to learn from failures and continue moving forward. Resilient teams are able to bounce back from setbacks, adapt to changing circumstances, and maintain their focus on their goals. Building resilience involves developing the skills and mindset needed to navigate challenges and persevere in the face of adversity. This might include fostering a growth mindset, encouraging flexibility and adaptability, and providing support and resources to help team members overcome obstacles.

Celebrating small wins and progress is an important practice that reinforces the value of learning from failures. By acknowledging and celebrating the incremental steps taken toward improvement, teams can maintain motivation and momentum. This recognition can take many forms, from formal awards and incentives to informal praise and acknowledgment. By celebrating progress, teams can reinforce the importance of learning and growth, inspiring team members to continue striving for success.

Continuous learning and development are essential for sustaining a culture of improvement. Teams must be committed to ongoing learning, seeking out new knowledge, skills, and perspectives that can enhance their performance. This might involve attending workshops, conferences, or training sessions, as well as encouraging team members to pursue their own learning and development goals. By fostering a culture of continuous learning, teams can stay at the forefront of their field and drive long-term success.

Incorporating feedback loops into the team's processes can enhance the ability to learn from failures. Feedback loops provide a mechanism for gathering input and insights from team members, stakeholders, and customers, allowing teams to make informed decisions and adjustments. By integrating feedback into their processes, teams can ensure that they remain responsive to changing needs and conditions, enhancing their ability to learn and improve.

Sustaining Long-Term Success

Sustaining long-term success in any team or organization requires a strategic approach that balances immediate achievements with future growth and adaptability. While reaching initial goals is a significant accomplishment, maintaining that success over time demands continuous effort, innovation, and resilience. By focusing on key principles and practices, teams can ensure their achievements endure and evolve in a rapidly changing environment.

A clear and compelling vision is the cornerstone of sustained success. This vision serves as a guiding star, providing direction and purpose for the team. It should be ambitious yet attainable, inspiring team members to strive for excellence while remaining grounded in reality. A well-articulated vision helps align individual and collective efforts, ensuring that everyone is working toward a common goal. Regularly revisiting and refining this vision can keep it relevant and motivating, adapting to new challenges and opportunities as they arise.

Adaptability is a crucial trait for sustaining success in a dynamic world. Teams must be prepared to pivot and adjust their strategies in response to changing circumstances, whether they be market shifts, technological advancements, or evolving customer needs. This requires a mindset that embraces change and views it as an opportunity for growth rather than a threat. Encouraging flexibility and innovation within the team can foster a culture of adaptability, enabling the organization to thrive in the face of uncertainty.

Continuous improvement is another key element of long-term success. Teams should be committed to regularly evaluating their performance, identifying areas for enhancement, and implementing changes that drive progress. This involves setting up mechanisms for feedback and reflection, such as regular reviews, performance assessments, and open discussions. By fostering a culture of continuous improvement, teams can ensure they remain competitive and relevant, consistently delivering value to their stakeholders.

Investing in talent development is essential for sustaining success over the long term. A skilled and motivated workforce is a critical asset, and organizations must prioritize the growth and development of their team members. This might involve providing training and development opportunities, offering mentorship and coaching, or creating pathways for career advancement. By nurturing talent, teams can build a strong foundation for future success, ensuring they have the skills and capabilities needed to meet evolving challenges.

Effective leadership is a driving force behind sustained success. Leaders must be visionary and strategic, guiding their teams with clarity and purpose. They should be adept at building strong relationships, fostering collaboration, and empowering team members to take ownership of their work. By modeling the values and behaviors they wish to see in their teams, leaders can inspire trust and commitment, creating a positive and productive work environment.

Building a strong organizational culture is vital for long-term success. Culture shapes the way team members interact, make decisions, and approach their work. A positive and inclusive culture fosters engagement, collaboration, and innovation, driving the organization toward its goals. Teams should be intentional about defining and nurturing their culture, ensuring it aligns with their values and vision. This might involve creating rituals and traditions, celebrating successes, and reinforcing desired behaviors.

Sustainability and social responsibility are increasingly important considerations for organizations seeking long-term success. Teams must be mindful of their impact on the environment and society, striving to operate in a way that is ethical and sustainable. This involves considering the long-term implications of business decisions, minimizing negative impacts, and contributing positively to the community. By prioritizing sustainability and social responsibility, teams can build trust and credibility with stakeholders, enhancing their reputation and long-term viability.

Effective communication is a fundamental aspect of sustaining success. Teams must ensure that information flows freely and transparently, enabling collaboration and informed decision-making. This involves establishing clear channels for communication, encouraging open dialogue, and actively listening to feedback. By fostering a culture of communication, teams can build strong relationships, resolve conflicts, and align their efforts toward common goals.

Case Studies Teams That Made History

Throughout history, certain teams have stood out for their remarkable achievements, leaving an indelible mark on their respective fields. These teams, through their innovation, collaboration, and perseverance, have not only achieved greatness but have also set benchmarks for others to follow. By examining these case studies, we can glean valuable insights into the dynamics and strategies that propelled them to success, offering lessons that can be applied to teams across various domains.

One of the most iconic teams in history is the Apollo 11 mission team, which successfully landed humans on the moon in 1969. This monumental achievement was the result of years of dedication, meticulous planning, and collaboration among thousands of scientists, engineers, and astronauts. The Apollo 11 team exemplified the power of a shared vision, as they worked tirelessly to fulfill President John F. Kennedy's ambitious goal of landing a man on the moon and returning him safely to Earth. The team's success was driven by their unwavering commitment to excellence, their ability to innovate under pressure, and their meticulous attention to detail. The Apollo 11 mission serves as a testament to the power of teamwork and the importance of setting clear, audacious goals.

Another remarkable team that made history is the Manhattan Project team, responsible for developing the first atomic bomb during World War II. This team, composed of some of the brightest minds in science and engineering, faced immense pressure to deliver a working weapon before the Axis powers. The Manhattan Project team demonstrated the importance of interdisciplinary collaboration, as experts from various fields came together to solve complex scientific and technical challenges. Their success was also a result of effective leadership, as figures like J. Robert Oppenheimer and General Leslie Groves provided direction and motivation to the team. While the ethical implications of their work continue to be debated, the Manhattan Project remains a powerful example of how a focused and well-coordinated team can achieve groundbreaking results.

In the realm of sports, the 1992 United States men's Olympic basketball team, known as the "Dream Team," is often cited as one of the greatest teams in history. Comprised of NBA legends such as Michael Jordan, Magic Johnson, and Larry Bird, the Dream Team dominated the competition, winning the gold medal with ease. The team's success was not only due to the individual talent of its members but also their ability to work together and complement each other's strengths. The Dream Team demonstrated the importance of chemistry and mutual respect, as players set aside their egos and personal rivalries to achieve a common goal. Their performance on the world stage elevated the global profile of basketball and inspired a new generation of players.

In the business world, the team behind Apple's resurgence in the late 1990s and early 2000s is a prime example of a team that made history. Under the leadership of Steve Jobs, Apple's team of designers, engineers, and marketers revolutionized the technology industry with products like the iMac, iPod, iPhone, and iPad. The team's success was driven by a relentless focus on innovation, design excellence, and user experience. Apple's team demonstrated the power of a strong vision and the ability to anticipate and shape consumer trends. Their work not only transformed Apple into one of the most valuable companies in the world but also changed the way people interact with technology.

The Human Genome Project, completed in 2003, is another historic achievement that showcases the power of teamwork. This international research effort aimed to map and understand all the genes of the human species, a task that required collaboration among scientists from around the world. The Human Genome Project team exemplified the importance of global cooperation, as researchers shared data, resources, and expertise to achieve a common goal. Their success has had a profound impact on the fields of medicine and genetics, paving the way for advances in personalized medicine and our understanding of human biology.

In the realm of social change, the Civil Rights Movement in the United States is a powerful example of a collective effort that made history. Led by figures such as Martin Luther King Jr., Rosa Parks, and John Lewis, the movement was driven by countless individuals and organizations working together to challenge racial segregation and discrimination. The success of the Civil Rights Movement was rooted in its ability to mobilize diverse groups of people, harness the power of nonviolent protest, and effect change through legal and legislative means. The movement's legacy continues to inspire social justice efforts around the world.

These case studies illustrate that while the contexts and challenges faced by each team were unique, there are common threads that run through their successes. A clear and compelling vision, effective leadership, interdisciplinary collaboration, and a commitment to excellence are key factors that contributed to their achievements. By studying these historic teams, we can gain valuable insights into the dynamics and strategies that drive success, offering lessons that can be applied to teams in any field.

Chapter 6

The Role of Leadership in Team Success

Leadership Styles and Their Impact on Teams

Leadership styles play a pivotal role in shaping the dynamics, culture, and performance of teams. The way a leader interacts with their team can significantly influence motivation, productivity, and overall success. Understanding different leadership styles and their impact on teams is crucial for anyone aspiring to lead effectively. By exploring various approaches, leaders can adapt their style to meet the needs of their team and the demands of the situation, fostering an environment where everyone can thrive.

One of the most well-known leadership styles is the autocratic style, characterized by a leader who makes decisions unilaterally and expects compliance from team members. This approach can be effective in situations where quick decision-making is essential, or when the leader possesses specialized knowledge that the team lacks. However, an autocratic style can also stifle creativity and innovation, as team members may feel disempowered and reluctant to share their ideas. To mitigate these drawbacks, autocratic leaders should strive to communicate openly and provide opportunities for team members to contribute their insights.

In contrast, the democratic leadership style emphasizes collaboration and participation. Democratic leaders actively seek input from team members and consider their opinions when making decisions. This approach fosters a sense of ownership and engagement, as team members feel valued and empowered to contribute. Democratic leadership can lead to higher morale and increased innovation, as diverse perspectives are considered. However, it can also result in slower decision-making processes, as reaching a consensus may take time. Leaders employing this style should balance inclusivity with efficiency, ensuring that decisions are made in a timely manner.

The transformational leadership style is centered around inspiring and motivating team members to achieve their full potential. Transformational leaders are visionary and charismatic, encouraging their teams to embrace change and pursue ambitious goals. This style can lead to high levels of motivation and commitment, as team members are inspired to go above and beyond. Transformational leaders often focus on personal development, providing mentorship and support to help team members grow. However, this style requires a high level of emotional intelligence and the ability to connect with team members on a personal level. Leaders should be mindful of maintaining authenticity and consistency in their vision and actions.

Transactional leadership, on the other hand, is based on a system of rewards and punishments. Transactional leaders set clear expectations and provide incentives for meeting goals, while also implementing consequences for failing to meet standards. This approach can be effective in environments where tasks are routine and well-defined, as it provides structure and clarity. However, transactional leadership may not be as effective in situations that require creativity and innovation, as it focuses on maintaining the status quo. Leaders using this style should ensure that rewards and consequences are fair and transparent, and consider incorporating elements of other styles to foster a more dynamic environment.

The servant leadership style prioritizes the needs and well-being of team members above all else. Servant leaders focus on supporting and empowering their team, fostering a culture of trust and collaboration. This approach can lead to high levels of satisfaction and loyalty, as team members feel genuinely cared for and valued. Servant leadership is particularly effective in environments where collaboration and teamwork are essential. However, leaders must be careful not to neglect their own needs or the strategic goals of the organization. Balancing the well-being of the team with the demands of the organization is key to the success of this style.

Laissez-faire leadership is characterized by a hands-off approach, where leaders provide minimal guidance and allow team members to make decisions independently. This style can be effective when team members are highly skilled and self-motivated, as it allows for autonomy and creativity. However, laissez-faire leadership can lead to a lack of direction and accountability if team members are not adequately supported. Leaders employing this style should ensure that team members have the resources and support they need to succeed, and be prepared to step in when necessary to provide guidance.

Situational leadership is a flexible approach that involves adapting one's leadership style to the needs of the team and the specific circumstances. Situational leaders assess the maturity and competence of their team members and adjust their style accordingly. This approach recognizes that there is no one-size-fits-all solution to leadership, and that different situations may require different approaches. By being adaptable and responsive, situational leaders can effectively guide their teams through a variety of challenges and opportunities.

Empowering Team Members Delegation and Trust

Empowering team members through effective delegation and trust is a cornerstone of successful leadership. When leaders delegate tasks and responsibilities, they not only distribute the workload but also foster an environment where team members feel valued and capable. Trust, on the other hand, is the glue that holds the team together, ensuring that delegation leads to empowerment rather than micromanagement. By mastering the art of delegation and cultivating trust, leaders can unlock the full potential of their teams, driving innovation and productivity.

Delegation begins with understanding the strengths and weaknesses of each team member. A leader must be attuned to the skills, experiences, and aspirations of their team to assign tasks that align with individual capabilities. This alignment ensures that tasks are completed efficiently and effectively, while also providing team members with opportunities for growth and development. By delegating tasks that challenge and stretch their abilities, leaders can help team members build confidence and competence.

Effective delegation requires clear communication. Leaders must articulate the objectives, expectations, and desired outcomes of the delegated task, providing team members with the information they need to succeed. This includes setting clear deadlines, outlining available resources, and specifying any constraints or limitations. By providing a comprehensive framework, leaders can empower team members to take ownership of their tasks, fostering a sense of accountability and responsibility.

While clarity is essential, leaders must also allow for autonomy and creativity. Micromanagement stifles innovation and undermines trust, as team members may feel that their abilities are not respected or valued. Instead, leaders should provide guidance and support while allowing team members the freedom to approach tasks in their own way. This autonomy encourages creative problem-solving and innovation, as team members are empowered to explore new ideas and approaches.

Trust is a fundamental component of effective delegation. Leaders must demonstrate trust in their team members' abilities and judgment, creating an environment where individuals feel confident in their roles. This trust is built through consistent and transparent communication, as well as by recognizing and celebrating team members' achievements. When team members feel trusted, they are more likely to take initiative, collaborate effectively, and contribute to the team's success.

Building trust requires vulnerability and openness from leaders. By admitting their own limitations and seeking input from team members, leaders can create a culture of mutual respect and collaboration. This openness fosters a sense of psychological safety, where team members feel comfortable sharing their ideas, concerns, and feedback. In such an environment, trust flourishes, and team members are more likely to engage fully and contribute their best efforts.

Feedback is a critical tool for empowering team members and reinforcing trust. Constructive feedback provides team members with insights into their performance, highlighting areas of strength and opportunities for improvement. Leaders should deliver feedback in a supportive and respectful manner, focusing on specific behaviors and outcomes rather than personal attributes. By providing regular and meaningful feedback, leaders can help team members grow and develop, reinforcing their confidence and competence.

Recognition and appreciation are powerful motivators that enhance empowerment and trust. By acknowledging team members' contributions and celebrating their successes, leaders can reinforce positive behaviors and foster a sense of belonging. Recognition can take many forms, from formal awards and incentives to informal praise and acknowledgment. By consistently recognizing and appreciating team members' efforts, leaders can create a positive and motivating work environment.

Empowerment through delegation and trust also involves providing opportunities for professional development. Leaders should encourage team members to pursue learning and growth, offering support and resources to help them achieve their goals. This might involve providing access to training programs, mentorship, or opportunities to take on new challenges and responsibilities. By investing in team members' development, leaders demonstrate their commitment to their growth and success, reinforcing trust and empowerment.

Leading by Example The Influence of Role Models

The influence of role models in leadership is profound, shaping not only the behavior and attitudes of team members but also the overall culture and success of an organization. Leading by example is a powerful tool that leaders can wield to inspire, motivate, and guide their teams toward achieving shared goals. When leaders embody the values, work ethic, and integrity they wish to see in their teams, they create a ripple effect that fosters trust, respect, and commitment.

At the heart of leading by example is authenticity. Authentic leaders are genuine and transparent, consistently aligning their actions with their words. This authenticity builds trust, as team members can rely on their leaders to be honest and dependable. When leaders are true to themselves and their values, they create an environment where team members feel safe to express their own authentic selves, fostering a culture of openness and inclusivity.

Integrity is another cornerstone of leading by example. Leaders who demonstrate integrity act with honesty and fairness, making decisions that reflect ethical principles and the best interests of the team. This integrity sets a standard for behavior within the organization, encouraging team members to uphold similar values in their own actions. When leaders consistently demonstrate integrity, they earn the respect and admiration of their teams, strengthening their influence and effectiveness.

Work ethic is a critical aspect of leading by example. Leaders who exhibit a strong work ethic demonstrate dedication, perseverance, and a commitment to excellence. By setting high standards for themselves, they inspire their teams to strive for similar levels of performance and achievement. A leader's work ethic can be contagious, motivating team members to put forth their best efforts and take pride in their work.

Empathy and compassion are essential qualities for leaders who wish to lead by example. By showing genuine concern for the well-being of their team members, leaders create a supportive and nurturing environment. Empathetic leaders listen actively, seek to understand the perspectives and needs of their team, and provide support and encouragement. This empathy fosters strong relationships and a sense of belonging, enhancing team cohesion and collaboration.

Resilience is a powerful trait that leaders can model for their teams. In the face of challenges and setbacks, resilient leaders maintain a positive attitude and demonstrate the ability to adapt and persevere. By showing resilience, leaders inspire their teams to remain focused and determined, even in difficult circumstances. This resilience can be a source of strength and motivation, helping teams navigate obstacles and emerge stronger.

Communication is a vital component of leading by example. Effective leaders communicate clearly and openly, sharing information and insights that empower their teams to make informed decisions. By modeling effective communication, leaders encourage team members to engage in open dialogue, share their ideas, and collaborate effectively. This communication fosters a culture of transparency and trust, enhancing team dynamics and performance.

Leaders who lead by example also prioritize continuous learning and development. By demonstrating a commitment to personal and professional growth, leaders encourage their teams to pursue their own learning and development goals. This might involve seeking out new knowledge, skills, and experiences, as well as being open to feedback and self-reflection. By modeling a growth mindset, leaders inspire their teams to embrace change and innovation, driving continuous improvement and success.

The impact of leading by example extends beyond the immediate team, influencing the broader organizational culture. When leaders consistently model the values and behaviors they wish to see, they create a culture that reflects those principles. This culture shapes the way team members interact, make decisions, and approach their work, driving the organization toward its goals. By leading by example, leaders can create a lasting legacy that influences the organization for years to come.

Coaching and Mentoring Developing Future Leaders

Coaching and mentoring are pivotal processes in developing future leaders, serving as the bridge between potential and performance. These practices not only enhance individual capabilities but also contribute to the overall growth and success of an organization. By investing in coaching and mentoring, leaders can cultivate a pipeline of talent ready to take on future challenges, ensuring the sustainability and resilience of their teams.

At the heart of effective coaching is the ability to guide individuals toward self-discovery and personal growth. Coaches act as facilitators, helping team members identify their strengths, weaknesses, and areas for development. This process often begins with setting clear and achievable goals, tailored to the individual's aspirations and the organization's needs. By establishing a roadmap for growth, coaches provide a sense of direction and purpose, motivating individuals to strive for continuous improvement.

Active listening is a fundamental skill for coaches, enabling them to understand the unique perspectives and challenges faced by their mentees. By creating a

safe and supportive environment, coaches encourage
open dialogue and honest reflection. This trust-based
relationship allows individuals to explore their
thoughts and feelings, gaining insights into their
motivations and behaviors. Through active listening,
coaches can provide targeted feedback and guidance,
helping individuals overcome obstacles and unlock
their potential.

Mentoring, on the other hand, involves a more
experienced individual sharing their knowledge, skills,
and experiences with a less experienced mentee. This
relationship is often characterized by a long-term
commitment, with mentors providing ongoing
support and encouragement. Mentors serve as role
models, demonstrating the values and behaviors they
wish to instill in their mentees. By sharing their own
experiences and lessons learned, mentors offer
valuable insights and perspectives that can accelerate
the development of future leaders.

One of the key benefits of mentoring is the
opportunity for mentees to gain exposure to different
viewpoints and approaches. By engaging with a
mentor, individuals can broaden their horizons and
challenge their assumptions, fostering a more holistic
understanding of their field. This exposure can inspire
creativity and innovation, as mentees learn to think
critically and adapt to new situations. Mentors can
also provide valuable networking opportunities,
introducing mentees to key contacts and resources
that can support their growth and development.

Both coaching and mentoring require a commitment to continuous learning and development. Coaches and mentors must stay informed about the latest trends and best practices in their field, ensuring they can provide relevant and up-to-date guidance. This commitment to learning extends to the individuals being coached or mentored, who should be encouraged to seek out new knowledge and experiences. By fostering a culture of learning, organizations can create an environment where future leaders are empowered to take initiative and drive change.

Feedback is a crucial component of both coaching and mentoring, providing individuals with insights into their performance and progress. Constructive feedback should be specific, actionable, and delivered in a supportive manner, focusing on behaviors and outcomes rather than personal attributes. By providing regular feedback, coaches and mentors can help individuals identify areas for improvement and celebrate their successes, reinforcing positive behaviors and building confidence.

The impact of coaching and mentoring extends beyond individual development, influencing the overall culture and success of an organization. By investing in these practices, organizations demonstrate their commitment to nurturing talent and fostering a supportive and inclusive environment. This commitment can enhance employee engagement and retention, as individuals feel valued and supported in their growth. Moreover, by developing a pipeline of future leaders, organizations can ensure

they are well-equipped to navigate future challenges
and opportunities.

Navigating Change and Uncertainty

Change and uncertainty are inevitable aspects of life,
particularly in the fast-paced and ever-evolving
landscape of modern organizations. Navigating these
challenges requires a blend of adaptability, resilience,
and strategic foresight. Leaders and teams must be
equipped with the tools and mindset necessary to
embrace change, mitigate risks, and seize
opportunities. By understanding the dynamics of
change and uncertainty, individuals can transform
potential obstacles into catalysts for growth and
innovation.

The first step in navigating change is recognizing its
inevitability and preparing for it proactively.
Organizations that anticipate change and plan
accordingly are better positioned to respond
effectively when it occurs. This preparation involves
conducting regular assessments of the external
environment, identifying potential trends and
disruptions that could impact the organization. By
staying informed and vigilant, leaders can develop
strategies that align with emerging opportunities and
challenges, ensuring their teams are ready to adapt.

Communication plays a critical role in managing
change and uncertainty. Transparent and timely
communication helps to alleviate anxiety and build
trust among team members. Leaders should provide

clear and consistent messages about the nature of the change, its implications, and the steps being taken to address it. By fostering an open dialogue, leaders can encourage team members to share their concerns and ideas, creating a collaborative environment where everyone feels involved in the change process.

Flexibility and adaptability are essential qualities for individuals and teams navigating change. The ability to pivot and adjust strategies in response to new information or circumstances is crucial for maintaining momentum and achieving success. Leaders should encourage a culture of experimentation and learning, where team members feel empowered to explore new approaches and take calculated risks. This mindset fosters innovation and resilience, enabling teams to thrive in the face of uncertainty.

Resilience is the capacity to recover from setbacks and maintain focus in challenging situations. Building resilience involves developing coping strategies and support systems that help individuals manage stress and maintain a positive outlook. Leaders can support resilience by promoting work-life balance, providing access to resources and training, and fostering a supportive and inclusive team culture. By prioritizing well-being and resilience, organizations can enhance their ability to navigate change and uncertainty effectively.

Scenario planning is a valuable tool for preparing for change and uncertainty. This process involves envisioning a range of possible future scenarios and developing strategies to address each one. By considering different outcomes and their potential impacts, organizations can identify opportunities and risks, allowing them to make informed decisions and allocate resources effectively. Scenario planning encourages strategic thinking and flexibility, equipping teams with the foresight needed to navigate complex and uncertain environments.

Empowerment and autonomy are critical components of successful change management. When team members feel empowered to take ownership of their roles and contribute to decision-making, they are more likely to embrace change and adapt effectively. Leaders should provide opportunities for team members to develop their skills and take on new responsibilities, fostering a sense of agency and accountability. This empowerment not only enhances individual performance but also strengthens the overall resilience and adaptability of the team.

Building a culture of continuous improvement is essential for navigating change and uncertainty. Organizations that prioritize learning and development are better equipped to adapt to new challenges and seize opportunities. Leaders should encourage a growth mindset, where team members are motivated to seek out new knowledge and skills, and where mistakes are viewed as opportunities for learning and growth. By fostering a culture of continuous improvement, organizations can enhance their agility and responsiveness in the face of change.